KERRY'S CHILDREN

A JEWISH CHILDHOOD IN NAZI GERMANY
AND GROWING UP IN SOUTH WALES

ELLEN DAVIS

seren

Seren is the book imprint of
Poetry Wales Press Ltd
Nolton Street, Bridgend, CF31 3BN, Wales
www.seren-books.com

ISBN 1-85411-371-2

A CIP record for this title is available from
the British Library.

The publisher works with the financial assistance of the
Welsh Books Council.

Printed in Plantin by CPD (Wales), Ebbw Vale.

Contents

Preface

I NEED TO EXPLAIN that the names of my family are the names I used as a child. My mother's father, my grandfather, was Herman Kaiser, known to me as Opa. My grandmother was Amelia known as Oma. My father, Julius Wertheim, was Papa and my mother Hannah was Mutti. These are the names I used then, and in my heart and mind still use.

Having introduced my Opa and Oma Kaiser, I must now introduce Papa's parents. My Opa Wertheim I do not remember at all. He died when I was only three years old. My memory of this event is of a long journey strapped to Papa's back whilst he rode an ancient motorbike. My Oma Wertheim I recall all too vividly. Although we saw her seldom, as young as I was, I remember her active dislike, which became mutual. In later years, I realised that she did not like any female, and this included Erika (her daughter and my aunt), who was only two years older than me. I remember Erika vividly, because of always having to wear her discarded clothes. Both my grandparents had seven children. The Kaiser family was made up of five boys and two girls, Mutti being the eldest. The Wertheim family had six boys and one girl, Erika. Papa was the second eldest of his family.

Part One
Germany

Before

THE LITTLE VILLAGE OF HOOF was on the main road to Kassel. This was the longest, most important road in the village. It had a wide carriageway with apple trees from which you could pick fruit, if you were tall enough, or pick up from the ground if you were small like me. The trees on one side were public property and everyone was allowed to pick the fruit. The other side of the road was very different. These trees were enclosed by wire and were private property. Those were the trees I loved. It was a case of forbidden fruit, no fun to pick what was allowed. Far more fun to steal from under or over the wire; how much tastier were these apples and what joy to pick, especially if you were not caught.

The wire enclosed an estate, for that is what it must have been. I recall a big house with a farm attached. During my early years, 1932 to '33 when I was three, I was sent daily to the big house for eggs and milk. I remember vividly a large metal can with a lid, which was almost as big as I was. Now I cannot imagine how I could have carried this together with a basket for the eggs. Each time I went to the house I was petrified, not of dogs or cats but of the guards, and what beautiful guards they were, but how vicious. They were glorious, their feathers were the colour of the rainbow. A delight to look at, if they allowed you the time to stop and stare. Mostly it was a case of getting to the house without being pecked. They were not fussy whom they chased, man, woman or child. Again and again I was scared. This in itself was strange, for before I had never known fear.

Where the grounds of the big house ended, the road continued climbing up the hill. This road was parallel with the one on which we lived. It wound its way upwards. On either side there were very tall houses. The first I remember was the bakery where each Friday Oma would take the twisted loaves and cakes to be baked. The smell of new baked bread still makes my mouth water. The other houses wandered up the hill till just one house stood way back from the road. It had a very small window in which little could be seen. This was the Jewish grocers. Once inside, the shop seemed to go on for ever. Like the bakery, the smells were tantalising. We children stood in the doorway attracted like bees to honey. The name of the grocer was Katz, I remember. The shop was end on to the road to the forest. If you turned left this would take you to the entrance to the big house where the peacocks frightened me so. To the right the road led into the forest. This was also the road to a large clearing where later the soldiers made their camp. Opposite the road into the forest and the grocery shop was the main Beer Garden and Dance Hall where each evening the villagers gathered. Also the place where we saw the bear dancing. I have a very vague memory of it. I must have been very young, watching Mutti and Papa dancing. I'm sure I did not imagine this; it's a vivid memory buried very long ago.

Beyond the Beer Garden, a small road led to the synagogue. A small but very beautiful building. Like all synagogues, ours had a downstairs, the most beautiful part. This was only for men and boys. Females sat in the gallery upstairs and took no physical part in the service, except of course singing at the appropriate time. The most impressive part of the synagogue (not just ours but all synagogues) is the place called the Bima. A raised platform where the main prayers are said and where the Torah is read. These are the Holy Books which contain the five books of Moses. Yet they are not really books at all but scrolls wrapped in embroidered velvet covers with breastplates of silver on which hangs a silver hand used to indicate the words which are read from the Tora. The Torah is the most holy and revered part of the synagogue. Just past the synagogue was the village square. At the time it seemed enormous, when I saw it sixty years later, it was just large enough to hold four cars.

My life was very sheltered, for we lived in a family house, in fact two houses made into one for our large family. This was Opa's house and besides Opa there was Oma, a number of uncles who made so little impression on me that I cannot recall their names, Papa and Mutti and by 1932 I had two brothers, Rolf, who was a year younger than I, and Heinz, who was two years younger. Quite a house full but the very numbers made for a lot of love and affection. Opa was a very tall soldierly looking man, who walked straight-backed; he had white hair and a most intriguing pair of glasses. One of the lenses was normal and the other was black. I discovered many years later that he had lost the sight of the right eye in the First World War, ironically fighting for the Germans. It did not seem to matter then that he was Jewish.

Oma was a little lady as small as Opa was tall. When I recall her I always think of her as white. She was as plump as a partridge, always in her large white pinafore and her hair was snowy white. As loving as only grandmothers can be. She was always there for us. If we fell or hurt ourselves, it was to Oma we ran. She would open her arms and kiss away the pain; in her arms there was love and safety. The uncles I do not recall except that they were part of the household. Papa was very tall to one as small as me, in fact he was about 5ft 9, very well built, with blonde curly hair, very handsome. A man who, like Opa, wanted to be in command. This he could only do with Mutti and us children. He was rather vain and enjoyed showing off his muscular body. Mutti was very slender, when not pregnant, shy, perhaps timid, a lovely face that always looked very serene. Her hair, which was darker than Papa's, she wore in a bun. She was a very lovely and loving wife and mother, adored by everyone. Her kindness knew no bounds, both to her family and to anyone in need.

She was a most obedient wife. Papa who was, like Opa ,very domineering, was to Mutti a God sent to earth just for her. Whatever Papa said Mutti would agree with him, right or wrong. Had he said the moon was made of blue cheese, Mutti would have said 'Yes Julius.' I have no recollection of ever hearing a disagreement, but that does not mean there were not any. My brothers were just babies I looked after. I was a little mother at three.

Opa was a very important person in the Jewish community. He was the butcher, known in Hebrew as the Sharot. Animals have to be killed in a special way and Opa, as the Sharot, not only killed the animals but also sold the meat. He, together with Papa and the uncles, would not only supply the community of Hoof, but would leave the village when it was still dark to drive to Kassel where in the market they put up a stall from which Jewish people of the town would buy their Kosher meat.

Opa also had a little shop attached to the house where he sold meat to our community. I remember this shop so vividly for it had a most intriguing machine that I loved. It was a machine that made sausages. In would go the meat and out would come a long round string of these strange things. I could never work out how it was done but I was fascinated by the process. Strange the things a child remembers.

In the garden of our house, there was a small stream. Playing in the water was the ultimate joy for me. Whenever I went missing, it was Opa who would find and haul me out of the stream, just as a puppy is carried by the scruff of the neck. He would wag his finger at me and forbid my going anywhere near the stream, but always with a twinkle in his eye.

As the first grandchild in the family I was much loved and I responded with great affection in return. When Rolf was born in December 1930, I was only a year old and loved him as I would a doll, a thing I never had. A while later, in June 1932, Heinz was born and I loved him just as much, except he was a crying baby which would upset me no end. Having grown up so close to nature I must have known a little something of how babies were made. I watched Mutti grow bigger and bigger and knew that a new baby was coming. To begin with, I wondered if it had anything to do with chocolates. The only time we had these was the day each baby was born. We were sent to play with other members of the family and on our return we had to go to the wood shed and there we'd find a chocolate whirl which indicated that another baby had arrived. In retrospect I realise that I never felt any jealousy, not aged two, three or any other time. I just loved these babies and loved to mother them, even when I was very young, a habit which never left me.

We were a very close family and our Jewishness was a big part of our lives – not that we ever gave it much thought. Opa as always took the lead. We went to the synagogue on Saturday as naturally as we breathed. Saturday was a very special day. Opa spent most of the day, as he spent any spare time he had, studying the Torah. To be a Sharot , he had to be almost as well versed in the Torah as a Rabbi. We were not allowed to do any of the things we would do in the week. Friday was a big day in the kitchen; Oma and Mutti would be cooking on a very funny stove. It was big and square and the smells from it so very tantalising. Oma would make bread and cakes, and would take them across the road to the local baker. The whole village did this. It was fascinating to see the big paddles pushing uncooked bread and cakes into the big oven. When we returned home sometime later with our Chales, special plaited loaves made especially for Friday night, we sat around the big table with its snowy white tablecloth. The table groaned with food, but first Oma would light the candles and Opa would say the prayer over the bread and wine and give each member of the family a piece of Chale dipped in salt and a very small sip of wine. After this the meal would begin. No dishes were washed and no other work was allowed to be done. In the winter the lights were switched on before the Sabbath, but we were not even allowed to switch them off. The lady next door would come in to feed the stove, wash the dishes and turn off the lights. We all went to the synagogue on Saturday morning. When we came home the lady next door would come and take the food out of the little oven and we would have our Sabbath meal. Again no washing of dishes until the sun had set. During this very long day we were not allowed to play or go out in case we did anything that could be forbidden on the Sabbath, which seemed to include almost anything. No one ever thought of complaining. Why should we, this was as normal as breathing. But we knew that if Opa was not working or sleeping, he would be studying his books, as did every Jewish man – always excepting Papa.

Papa did not really fit into our Jewish part of the family. He went his own way, and nothing anyone said to him would make a jot of difference. He held himself accountable to no-one. A strange man, my Papa, though this of course is hindsight. He loved my Mutti dearly and equally he loved his children, but still he went his own way. He was supposed to be working for Opa, but I have a feeling he did little work. He loved to go with his friends to a local hall where they practised bodybuilding. He certainly was a very handsome man. I have photographs that prove it. He looked every bit the perfect German. I believe he was German first and Jewish merely by birth. On special occasions he would come to the synagogue with us, but these were few and far between. Papa was liked by all and had many friends, mainly non-Jewish. His best friend was the local policeman, whom we called uncle. They did their bodybuilding together, played cards with other friends and this was the sort of life that suited him. However much he loved his children and adored Mutti, nothing was allowed to interfere with what he wanted to do.

I adored my Papa, but as young as I was could see his faults. It was a strange relationship. From a very early age, I knew that Papa was responsible for Mutti's pain and discomfort. This made for a love-hate relationship between Papa and me. He of course knew nothing of my feelings. Each time Mutti was pregnant, her legs caused her the worst pain. She had very bad varicose veins. I would watch her legs each day. When I saw the veins appear I would tell her that there was going to be another baby. Each time this happened she would give me a very bemused look saying 'Child how can you know?' I would point to her legs and tell her 'Mutti, look at your legs.' I loved babies but felt each and every one of her pains. As the pregnancy advanced, her walking became unbearable, but she would never give in despite the pain. She was who she was and had to do what had to be done. As wife and mother there was no one to equal her. Papa could not have been an easy man to live with, yet her love and adoration of him knew no bounds. I wish I could say that he appreciated this, but, as I have said, he just took things for granted and as his right.

The days before 1933 were happy and contented. Thankfully

we did not know what the future held. Strange memories of that time come flooding back. The kitchen where one and all congregated around a square tiled stove, which had little pipes coming out in all directions, the forerunner of central heating. I can see Opa and Oma sitting of an evening with wires sticking out of their ears, and realise that as backward as the village was, we must have had a crystal set radio. No one else was allowed to use this instrument. Opa had laid down the law. It must have been very early in my life. The kitchen was for many things, not just cooking. It was a gathering place for the family. Above the stove was a series of shelves. In the winter we children were put there in feather duvets and a pillow, and there we slept.

It is strange that I tend to remember only two seasons, summer and winter. The summer very hot, the time when I loved my little stream most. The winter was the time for Papa to bring out the toboggans. Hoof, our little village, was at the bottom of a mountain and on the edge of a forest. How high those hills were and what fun to come screaming with delight down them. Not much fun having to drag the toboggan up, but we were a tough bunch and thought little of dragging the thing up the steep hill, it was merely a nuisance. In our stable was a very old horse, snow white and mine to ride whenever I wanted, but I wonder now why this lovely horse was kept alive. Opa was always practical and only useful animals were given house room. How I loved that horse – and now realise that was why it was kept. One winter day I was riding Snowy. There was ice on the road and the horse slipped, broke a leg and to my horror had to be put down. Not in front of me, thank heaven. Opa would not have allowed this to happen in front of me. I was never a crying child but on this occasion broke my heart and cried as if I had lost a dear friend.

In my mind I have a picture of a special occasion. It was spring. The time for Passover. This was a great family occasion when uncles and aunts would come to gather in Hoof. The house had first to be cleaned, every inch of it. Opa would go around with a large feather and dustpan, and heaven help anyone if he found a crumb of bread. When he was at last satisfied, all the dishes in daily use were packed into big crates, put into the attic and the Passover things would be brought out. Not just dishes and cutlery but saucepans and all implements used for cooking – and I mean all. The great day arrived. The door between the kitchen and living room (I do not remember anyone living in this room) was removed and every chair in the house was set around an enormous table, which I now realise was more than one table. In the place of honour at the head of the table was set an armchair padded with pillows which Opa as head of the family sat in in splendour. The table was a thing of joy. All the china and glass gleamed and shone. I wish I could remember how many of the family were present, but cannot. Only know that no matter how far away any of the uncles lived they had to return for Passover. This was Opa's decree and was obeyed. The next evening and the first part of the Seder, the name of this, came and I had a part to play. With shaking knees I would get up and ask three questions, in Hebrew of course. I cannot remember a time when I did not know Hebrew; we learned it at the little Jewish school where we went twice a week. When my ordeal was over the wine was drunk, four glasses for the first part. We children, of course, were only given a sip and did not like it. When the interval came, the food, which had been prepared for days, was put on the table which groaned with the wonderful dishes. The smell was heavenly. After the meal the last part of the Seder was finished. The children were fast asleep by this time but were not allowed to leave the table till Opa said amen. I can see the table now and smell the wonderful food. It is the enormous snowy white tablecloth that is the most vivid memory.

Things Change

IN THE VILLAGE every child of my age was a friend. Children do not question religion or the beliefs of others. I knew that I was Jewish and went to the synagogue on Saturday and knew also that some of my friends did the same and others went to church on Sunday. So what? This was subconscious knowledge, not something that any of us thought about. We were friends and spent a great part of each day playing together. No child thinks in terms of religion, it is something that is taken for granted as part of life and no distinction is made.

The joy of my happy life was another thing I took for granted. Then, towards the end of 1933 everything changed, not gradually, but almost overnight. One night knowing my Opa and Oma were out and Mutti in bed, once again pregnant, I heard voices downstairs and being a nosy child went down to see who the visitor was talking to Papa. I did not dare go into the kitchen, Papa would not have approved and taken his belt to me. The door was not quite closed. I saw our uncle, the policeman and Papa's best friend. Heard him say 'Julius please do not speak to me when we meet in the street or for that matter at any time in the future. I have to wear this awful armband and dare not be seen talking to a Jew.' He added, 'Please tell the children they must no longer call me uncle and if I am or seem to be cross with them tell them I do not mean it. My job and family have to come first and as much as it hurts me I have to conform to this Nazi policy.' When he had finished, they both burst out crying. What had been said was beyond my comprehension. I did not know that men could cry and it was a great shock to see this. Next morning Papa tried very hard to make us children understand what our uncle had told him. To us of course it made no sense at all. What was a Nazi? And why did our uncle say we must not talk to him? We soon found out the hard way.

Hitler had come to power. The leader of the Nazi Party had become Chancellor of Germany. It must be remembered that this was no ordinary man, but a megalomaniac. He took a country which was bankrupt, where most of the men who had lost the First World War were without work and put the idea into their heads that he was the Messiah who would lead them into what he called 'The Third Reich'. In this utopia there would be work for all and food on every table. He took men out of the gutter, the lowest of the low, put them into uniforms, originally just an arm band, and made them believe they were a new army. An army of thugs, murderers who did his bidding and worshiped him and his great ideas. He made his new army believe that all their troubles had been caused by Jews. The Jews, he said, had all the money and therefore were responsible for the poverty and trouble Germany was in. In the 1920s he had written a book called *Mein Kampf* in which he had set out what he wanted Germany to become, completely Aryan. People must have blonde hair and blue eyes and conform to a pattern. The stupid part of this was the fact that he himself was not German, but Austrian. He did not have blonde hair or blue eyes, yet wanted to build a world to conform to these ideals. The worst part of the book was that he had planned the extermination of all Jews, mainly to confiscate their property and monies. The noncon-forming of the Jews with their dark hair and brown eyes was a red herring. The Jews became his scapegoats and very useful ones they turned out to be. Hitler promised a Jew-free Germany, his Third Reich could not and would not tolerate Jews. Their termination was a major part of his overall plan. Even before he became Chancellor he had already had built the first concentra-tion camps. As early as 1930, at the least excuse, Jews were taken into these places of terror and treated like animals. Strangely, Hitler was not against the emigration of Jews. At a price. One could buy one's way out of the camps on the condition that the man and his family left Germany within six weeks leaving behind all properties and monies. The people who could afford to do this naturally left the country as soon as humanly possible. They were the lucky ones. Hitler set up his Nazi army complete with his own police, and to police these he set up the Gestapo. These... what can I call them? Not animals, animals do not terrorize, hurt and treat their own species as the Gestapo treated Jews, and at times even Germans. The people who did not follow Hitler like sheep and worship him, these too were sent to concentration camps. This was Germany after 1933.

All the friends we had and had known all our young lives suddenly turned into enemies. They had become young Nazis. Instead of playing with us they shunned us and then started to call us names. To me the worst name, which they kept repeating, was 'Dirty Jew.' I would run home and ask Mutti why they had called me dirty? I was no dirtier than I had been the day before.

Of course I knew I was Jewish, so nothing made sense any more. Poor Mutti, there was no way to explain Hitler's dictates to a four year old. Papa was no help. At the best of times he was not a patient man, but now he was completely helpless. There is no way a child can comprehend such a turn about way of life. Nothing had changed and yet everything had changed. It was when they, the other children, started to throw stones at us and physically attack us that Papa thought it was time something was done. It was now 1934 and I was 5 years old. This something was teaching me, a five-year-old girl, to box and fight. After all I was the eldest and it was my duty to look after my younger brothers aged four and three. To me it made sense. I could not allow Rolf and Heinz to be hurt. How many times had Papa taken off his belt and strapped me with it. I was the eldest and was responsible for any scratch or hurt they may have suffered. Wasn't I in charge of them and wasn't it my duty to look after them. I had never thought how unjust my punishment was as I always took it in my stride. But now it was very different, this was serious, as were the lessons in boxing and fighting. I must have been a good pupil, although Papa was the last person to ever admit this. I remember on many occasions coming home with a split lip or a black eye. The only comment from Papa was 'What did the other child look like?' I never told him that rarely was it one child, they roamed and attacked in numbers and I was too obstinate to run away, would make my brothers run home but I would stand and fight. It was so very awful and strange to have to fight these one time friends. Even the girls who so recently would come to our house to admire the babies and stay for cakes and the fruit drink that only Oma could make. This was a strong enticement for any child. She would take all sorts of fruit, squeeze the juice and mix with water. What a treat. I had a special friend, my age, called Gretel. We were inseparable when I was not busy with the babies. She was blonde and had blue eyes. So what, I too was blonde with blue eyes and my plaits were longer than hers. We would measure the length of our plaits – a contest I always won. We spent many hours together playing mothers with the babies, or collecting walnuts from under a wonderful large tree at the edge of the forest. Her parents were friends of ours and there were times we all went on picnics together. Never very far, there were no cars available. It was taken for granted each family brought their own food. We were Jewish and our food was different, though not in any big way. We just did not mix meat with milk and little things like that. Nobody cared. Why should they, it had always been that way. Now it had all gone, all the fun of playing with our friends, swapping marbles, playing with small stones which we had to pick up onto the backs of our hands. Just having friends to play with, all gone.

The only fear I had in my life up to then was the fear of the peacocks. Now fear became an everyday thing. Not just fear of the little monsters we had called friends, but fear of words we did not know the meaning off. Dachau, Hitler, concentration camp. What was a concentration camp ? From time to time Papa mysteriously would go away to a place called Dachau and it would be a long time before he returned and, then, only for a very short time. What was Dachau? A word spoken or rather whispered. He would never tell us but we always heard Mutti crying when he returned home and harder when he left. Over the years I came to equate his short time spent at home with my Mutti again being pregnant. By now there was another word and men we feared, the Gestapo. Very tall men, made to look taller by their jack boots and the caps they wore with such pride and arrogance. They always looked angry especially when they saw us. We would see them coming in their long leather coats, jackboots and caps with the badge of a Deathshead on the front. Then I would run away in fear, herding my brothers in front of me, so that they came to no harm. How I came to hate as well as fear these monsters. Their greatest joy was to hurt someone who could not hurt back, not that anyone could hurt them anyway. They were the Gestapo and above the law, such as it was. It was they who would make their own laws and carry out the wishes of Hitler, a name so hated and not only by Jews. There were many non-Jews who hated his decrees. Unfortunately they could do nothing to help us, for then their lives would also be in danger.

The anti-Jewish feeling became so strong that, eventually, no one spoke a word to us, but looked at us as if we shouldn't even exist. We had even come to fear our Uncle Fritz the policeman. Yet one look into his eyes, I was not frightened, and I understood what he could not say. I would see the uncle who was going completely against his nature, but that was the way he had to behave. There were many people who had been friends of our family. Mutti and Papa as well as Opa and Oma had always been very much-admired people. They were always generous and treated one and all as friends. These same people were now enemies, enemies in a big way, not because they wished to be, but to safeguard their own families.

How is it possible to explain to a child the difference between the Gestapo, who thank heavens never spoke to us, but looked at us with hatred in their eyes, and other people who were once friends but were now enemies, not because they hated us, they didn't. It was just not safe to show affection for a Jew. It was not safe, and safety was paramount for themselves and their families.

Experiences to a child are vivid and even to this day unforgettable. The daily onslaught of goose-stepping soldiers heard in the distance and coming ever nearer, going to their training ground at the other end of the village, became a sound of menace. Despite this we were children and our curiosity was no different from any other child's. We would follow at a safe distance, eager to see what the little trailer behind the last lorry contained. It was always there behind the last lorry. We learned that it was a little kitchen. We could smell the food which would make our mouths water, even though we knew it would be forbidden to us. We watched always at a distance. Afraid that the soldiers would see us. Had they done so they would have offered sweets. We could not take a chance on being seen. There were other children there who knew us and would have told the soldiers that we were Jewish. What would the soldiers do then? This thought filled us with fear. But the aura surrounding these soldiers was more than fear. It was menace and evil. Even now I can hear the sound of the goose-step, the smack of leather on the cobbles, the rattle of lorries and gun carriages. The 'strutting peacocks' marched with such pride. Any excuse to fling their arms out in the Nazi salute. Even more frightening was the song they sang as they marched. It was called the 'Horst Wessel Song'. I cannot recall, or perhaps am afraid to recall, all the words. It started 'When Jewish blood on my knife flashes then I feel oh so happy.' A very rough translation as I no longer speak German.

School

WHEN I WAS FIVE YEARS OLD I went to school. I had been looking forward to it for a long time. On the morning of this memorable day, Mutti presented me with a very large cornucopia made of cardboard and made very pretty with fancy paper. This was a present every child received on first going to school. Inside the beautiful cone were small gifts of fruit, sweets (a great treat), pencils and all sorts of goodies. Carrying this joyful gift off I went. As our village was so small, the school consisted of only two rooms. Before lessons started, all the children stood in the schoolyard to watch the swastika being raised on the flagstaff. While this took place every child stood to attention with arm stretched out in the Hitler salute, singing the new national anthem. We Jewish children were, of course, not allowed to be present during this ceremony. They didn't seem to realise how much we would have hated to participate? The ceremony completed, all the children, including us, returned to our schoolrooms, I, of course, for the first time. What a disappointment this longed for day turned out to be. All the Jewish children were made to sit at the back of the class, isolated from the other children as if we had a contagious disease.

No one spoke to us, not the teacher, nor any of the children. We learned what we could from copying what was on the blackboard; this was little enough when we could not ask a question or request an explanation. I can remember a film shown to the school. It was *The Pied Piper of Hamelin*. I cannot understand how we Jewish children were allowed to watch this, for we were not allowed anything that could give us pleasure. I have so few memories of school days. Break times we had to remain in the classroom in case we came into contact with the other children and contaminated them – I heard that phrase but had no idea what it meant. Lunch time I went home to have a snack with my family, always reluctant to return to school, always knowing return was inevitable. After a year Rolf joined me in the isolation

25

in the back of the classroom. But I think his life was made even more miserable than mine. He was a quiet, sensitive boy, hating rows or even harsh words. I was the tough one. Lessons were bad enough but after school, oh, that was different, the harassment started and how. Age, sex, size did not come into it. We were spat on, pinched, stoned, pushed and chased almost to our door by children of all ages. What I could not cope with was the fact that these had been my friends since I could remember, and now they were enemies.

In 1935 when I was just six and Rolf five and a half, Hitler made his Nuremberg Decree. No Jewish child to attend a German school. No Jewish lawyer to practise except for Jews. No doctor to attend Germans, no teacher to teach other than Jewish children. In shops cards appeared reading 'Jews only'. Parks, swimming pools, all recreation places, NO JEWS ALLOWED. Hitler had decreed and woe betide any German seen in a Jewish shop. Strangely the school part quite pleased me. I had this longing to learn. Although I did manage to learn to read, I did not learn to write until I was ten years old and in a different world. School was hell for both Rolf and me, we desperately wanted not to have to return each day. But Papa was adamant, 'It is important that you learn as much as you can, so back to school with the pair of you'. As always his word was law until Hitler's decree came into force which was the end of so very much, and more than we knew.

Fear

DEAR OPA was a very strong family man. During the years of Hitler's Nuremberg Law of 1935 no Jew could carry on any business; the business was confiscated. This upset Opa badly. His business had been taken away. How was he to feed his large family? Opa was in despair. He went to Kassel almost daily, never discussing what he had done there when we children were in the room. We eventually found out. He had been making enquiries about emigrating. The only place he thought we could all go to was Argentina. It seemed the only place for which he would have enough money for the passage. One day he came home smiling and hugging Oma.

The talk was of this wonderful place called Argentina. There we would all find peace. The men would work, there was a lot of space in this place, and of course they would need a Sharot and butcher, so no worry on that score. We children would all have horses to ride, for there were many horses there. I have no idea where Opa found this information, the only thing I had ever seen him read was the newspaper, even that was long before the talk of Argentina and Emigration. He had stopped reading the paper a long time ago.

One day, after many trips to Kassel, Opa and Oma contacted all the family. There was no telephone, so it must have been by telegram. Soon they all arrived. Normally, children were excluded from family conferences. This time Opa insisted that Rolf and I be present. A bit scary, this was after all a first for us. He talked in a very choked voice, explaining that he had tried so very hard to find passage for us all to our now hoped for 'paradise', my word not his. He had actually found a ship that was willing to take passengers to Argentina. He told us how pleased he had been, that is until the cost was discussed. Then the axe fell. There was not enough money for all of us to make the trip. I had never seen my Opa in tears, yet here he was trying to speak and having to stop every few minutes to wipe his eyes.

What it amounted to was: the money the family had, was only sufficient for Opa, Oma, three uncles and our aunt. None of the uncles or the aunt had ever made any impression on us. Sometimes they were there, other times we never gave them a thought. But there was only enough money for six people. He kept saying 'What can I do, where can I turn?' Because people were so very anxious to leave Germany, places on ships were very scarce. This had been the last ship, at the time, to accept passengers to Argentina. That was why poor Opa had been forced to accept the places for the members of the family who were going and to pay the money there and then. There was really nothing to discuss, the decision had of necessity been made.

A few weeks later, after a great deal of packing, crying, packing and crying, all the trunks were packed. There seemed so many of them. One morning, Papa brought our lorry to the front door. He and the uncles loaded all the trunks and bags, and suddenly without another word he drove away. A little while later a large car came to the house. After much crying, sobbing and many good-byes, Opa said, 'As soon as we can make enough money, we will send for all of you.'

I did so want to believe him, but as the car drove away, somehow I knew in my heart that I would never see them again. No, this is not hindsight; it was something I felt at the time. Unfortunately, it turned out I was only too right.

How empty the house was after six of our family had left. True they had not all lived with us. It was Oma and Opa who were forever absent. All we children, and I am sure Mutti too, went about the house praying that it had all been a nightmare. Unfortunately it was only too real. We were alone. Even more than before, it was to me my family turned. That sounds strange, but it had always been to me the children turned for things, large or small. For the changing of a nappy, a cut finger, or merely when they were hungry. Poor Mutti. After all her child bearing she was exhausted, now there was no Oma to cook and do the housework. I had always looked after my children, but Oma had always been there to turn to. Mutti, whom I loved beyond words, was not a mother to me, but just another child, all but helpless. She was always tired and as hard as she tried to do her share, it was just too much for her. I had to be the practical one, Rolf was the entertainer and his job was to keep the younger children occupied and quiet when they were in the house. How grateful we all were for the long garden. I seem to have left Papa out of this equation, deliberately. I do not think he knew what a nappy was, he was no help in the house, the kitchen or with the children. That is when he was home and not in Dachau. He was a man of his time. Housework and children were for women, men did not interfere, nor were they expected to take part in chores. I would love to have been able to read his mind. How could he expect a worn out wife and a seven-year-old girl to manage? I do not know the answer, but know he did.

It is time to write more about Papa. He was a great influence in my life, some good and some bad. He was a strange and selfish man. Loved Mutti and us children very dearly, but loved himself more. He never, if he could help, took any responsibility for anything. I think this must have been due to his working, such as it was, with Opa. Work and my Papa did not go well together. Even in the old days, I mean before life became too difficult to bear, he would work as little as he could get away with. His life consisted of making my Mutti pregnant and his bodybuilding, which he loved, and playing cards. In the old days he would vanish for days and nights at a time. On his return there was never an explanation. We of course knew he would be with one of his friends, for they too were nowhere in sight.

My relationship with my Papa was very strange. I loved this tall, blonde, handsome man, even though he showed little interest in me or my siblings. On the other hand I hated him. At a very early age I knew where children came from. Not the mechanics, but, as I have said, I knew that when papa was around sooner or later Mutti's legs would swell and those terrible black grapes would appear. Of course I blamed Papa for the agony Mutti had to suffer and for this my hatred was very real. It was Papa who taught me about love and hate and many other things.

My Papa was both a complex and a naïve man. Because he thought of himself as German first and Jewish second, he was quite convinced that no matter what happened to others, nothing would ever happen to him. How wrong he was. Papa was a man who spoke first and thought after. Soon what happened to other Jewish men happened to him. He hated Hitler and all he stood for, and said so in public. I realise now, he must also have been rather stupid. Although he thought himself invincible, it never occurred to him to keep his thoughts and hatred to himself. Every man, woman and child was by this time so brainwashed that they would report to the Gestapo anything they had heard or overheard. The children would even report their own parents had a word of criticism been heard.

I think my Papa still believed in his so-called friends. Despite everything that happened to us children. He was soon to learn better. One of his disparaging remarks had been overheard by someone; it could even have been one of his so-called friends. The Gestapo came, beat him and sent him to Dachau, to this place whose name had always frightened us. It was a long time before we heard from him again.

I have been told over the years that men did not go in and out of Dachau. People have doubted me when I tell them this happened. It was many years before I heard the explanation. The Commandant of the concentration camp, for that was what Dachau was, was a great gambler. All supporters of Hitler believed as he did, that Jews were an inferior race, small and weak. In my Papa, he found an exception and this suited him fine. As early as 1934 the concentration camps were already being enlarged. The existing buildings added to and more barracks built, the work done by the prisoners including my Papa. The Commandant would bet with the other officers as to which Jew could carry the most bricks in a hod onto the roof. It was inevitable that the man chosen by the Commandant would be Papa. He was the strongest man in the camp and it was only politic that the officers took the bet of their Commandant. After a while, 'the Commandant's Jew,' as Papa came to be known, always won. To show his pleasure, this dreadful man would give Papa a week's leave. Just time enough for Papa to come home and make Mutti pregnant. This may sound very unfair, especially coming from a child. But it was the truth and I was the one who had to deal with the consequences. The varicose veins, which would cause Mutti such hellish pain, the morning sickness she used to try to hide but never could. All the pain and misery my poor Mutti uncomplainingly put up with. All this hurt me very badly and I was never able to forgive Papa for causing her this hell. It was very strange. It never occurred to Papa that someone had to look after his wife and children. Of course, I realise he had no choice in the going into and coming out of Dachau. But surely he could have taken a little care about making Mutti pregnant again. He was a very thoughtless man.

Time went by. I never thought if it went quickly or slowly, it just went. Each day much like the one before. Fear always present and caring for my Mutti and children as normal as breathing. Where had those wonderful days of freedom gone? Do I honestly remember the smell of the pine trees, remember Oma taking me into the forest looking for the largest anthill. When she found it she would roll up her sleeve, plunge her arm in while I would stand crying for her pain. It's only now that I realise the reason for her strange behaviour. She had very bad arthritis. I do remember. Oh, I do remember.

Just as I remember the hundreds of soldiers strutting grim faced to an out of tune 'Umpapa' band. They were surrounded by a smell so strong one could almost taste it. How could we have known that their training would one day be used in a war that killed millions of people. They so enjoyed putting fear into, not just Jews, but anyone who saw them. Their demeanour was so arrogant, their faces so grim, almost as if they knew what the future held for them. They considered themselves the "Master Race". Why not? Hitler had chosen them to be the future of Germany, the Aryan ideal.

Persecution

ONE NIGHT, Papa was again in Dachau, when two Gestapo men came to our house. They did not knock, even if the door was locked. I never remember a locked door. They came into the house, shouting at Mutti, 'We want your jewellery.' Poor lady, the only jewellery she had were her wedding ring which they took off her finger, and a tiny pair of coral earrings in her pierced ears. They did not stop to allow her to take them out of her ears, they tore them out. Shouting like lunatics, because they could find nothing else, they left the house. Rolf and I spent the rest of the night stopping the bleeding. All of us were petrified in case these monsters returned. Monsters they certainly were. They enjoyed inflicting pain; the more one cried the greater their enjoyment. We were so very proud of Mutti. She must have gone through hell but did not even murmur, until the monsters had left. Then of course she cried in sheer agony. This was not an isolated incident of 'enjoyment' for those monsters. They thrived on other people's pain. 'Other people' of course had to be Jews, otherwise where was the fun?

It was harrowing always waiting for something else to go wrong. We didn't have to wait very long. Thank heavens Papa was home when the Gestapo came once more. They said to Papa, 'This house is too good for Jews, out.' Not an hour's notice, but that minute. We took what we could, Papa heavily laden for we would not be able to return for anything else. Where were we to go? As we asked the question, we saw the answer. A dirty, lazy family, to whom before no one would even talk, had now come up in the world. The man of the family had joined the Nazi party. Now in uniform he really thought he was someone. Amazing what a uniform does. They had lived in a hovel, no other word for it, a dirty, filthy house with three rooms. You really could not even call it a house. The Gestapo had decided that this filthy family, now members of the Nazi party, was to have our house and we were to move into theirs.

It had been bad enough living in our lovely but lonely house on our own, but to leave our beloved home and to move into this awful place had us all in tears. We had no choice, so made the best of things. Within a week, Papa was once again back in Dachau. So it fell as usual to us children, to scrub, clean and make this hovel liveable. An almost impossible task, but we did it. You have never seen, or heard such quiet children. As always I was in charge, and gave Rolf the job of keeping the little ones occupied. We dared not go outside, except of course into the yard to wash and use their dirty toilet. There was nothing we could do about it, and at least we were together. Time passed slowly, our suffering great. Our house had been a luxurious home by comparison, where we found ourselves now was sheer hell.

Once again Papa was back with us when they came again, saying the same words, 'This house is too good for Jews.' We were in despair. We had put our hearts into cleaning this place to make it habitable. Now again we had nowhere to go. The Jewish community, as always, came to our rescue. The schoolroom at the rear of the synagogue was opened and mattresses were spread on the floor. All seven of us lived in this confined space. We were lucky. Next door to the schoolroom there was a very small room containing a toilet and washbasin and a little wood-burning stove. Before many days had passed Papa was sent back to Dachau again. We coped as well as possible, for what else could we do? The congregation must have fed us, for I have no idea where the food we ate came from. It was winter and we were always cold. We huddled together in our one room. Day after day, each one the same as the one before. We lived in fear, what else could happen to us? None of us had any idea.

These events happened in 1937 when I was eight years old. We children rarely went out of doors for we could not afford to have anything more happen to upset Mutti. She, poor lady, was a nervous wreck and as always I saw to the comfort, such as it was, of both her and the children. It is not possible to give a chrono-logical account of the days, weeks or months. We existed in the one room and thank heavens the children were neither the whining nor the crying kind. They were very good, well behaved and amazingly quiet. It paid to be quiet for we did not want to draw attention to ourselves. Despite making ourselves as incon- spicuous as possible our troubles were far from over. Yes, we had a roof over our heads, very, very cramped, and to my knowledge we did not lack food, but we lived in fear of what we did not know. Winter had come. No tobogganing for us now or any of the other fun we once enjoyed in the snow. Once again Papa was home. He had only been with us a few days, when hell broke loose.

It was a night in December 1937. Bitterly cold and snowing heavily. Suddenly Papa was shouting, 'Out, out quickly'. We awoke to his voice and immediately smelled smoke. Mutti picked up Ludwig, the baby, I grabbed Ruth, at the time my only sister. Papa, still shouting, made sure that we were all outside. Only then did we realise what had happened. The synagogue was on fire and burning strongly. The Hitler Youths, yobs in their fancy uniforms, had decided they wanted a bonfire. What better place than the synagogue. Our village was small enough for everyone to know that we, the Wertheim family, lived in the building. This made no difference to the junior monsters. I remember little of that night, but one memory stands out so very clearly. A line of Hitler youths facing the entrance of the synagogue holding bricks in their hands. They were waiting to stone us to death as we ran from the fire. Not supposition, fact. Confirmed many years later by the people who smuggled us away from the chaos and saved our lives. These kind people hid us in an ice cellar until morning. They were the owners of the Big House, where in years gone by the peacocks had so frightened me. They had no time for Hitler and his ideals. Their humanity was intact. Seeing a family they knew, in such dreadful circumstances, they acted. Our lives were saved by people who did not put their own safety first. They smuggled us away during the chaos. Took us to their home and hid us. In those days there were no fridges or freezers. To keep food fresh for any length of time, a large almost room-sized cavity was cut out of the nearest hill. Blocks of ice brought there during the winter, thus creating an ice house where goods were stored throughout the year. Here, where no-one thought of looking for us, we stayed safely through the night.

Morning came and our family was torn apart. Papa was sent back to Dacha, Mutti and Ludwig, five months old, were sent to a camp for destitutes, which was some eight to ten miles outside the nearest town Kassel and consisted of rows and rows of metal huts. The people who were sent there were many and varied. Criminals who wore green badges, Gypsies who wore brown badges, political prisoners whose badges were red. Jehovah's Witnesses whose badges were mauve. Homosexuals who wore pink and Jews who wore yellow star of David badges. Colours to make inmates immediately recognisable. All these people lived in metal huts separated into about ten foot long units. Each holding a family or a number of individuals. For every forty people there was a water pipe outside, just one pipe for all. One toilet again for the same number of people. Not quite a concentration camp, but not far off.

The rest of us, my brothers and my sister and I, were taken to Kassel and delivered to the Jewish Orphanage, to the "White House" as it was called.

The Orphanage

AS WE ARRIVED AT THE GATES a strange thing happened to me. I recalled, as a very small child, going with Mutti to this enormous house. We had come to collect Opa's new glasses. The optician lived here, an old man whose son and daughter-in-law were the Superintendents at the Orphanage. For an instant I was back as the little girl who had cried when her mother had explained that the children who lived here had no mother or father. Now here I was again with my brothers and sisters, but this time I was not afraid, I had Mutti and Papa even if they were not with us. There we five children stood. I, eight years old. Long blonde plaits, blue eyes, looking anything but Jewish. Rolf was seven, taller than I. His hair just a stubble, a gentle boy. Heinz was six, and looked very like Rolf but a more belligerent child. Hair cut like his brother's. Sally was four. He was always called Bubbie, no idea why. He, unlike the other boys, had ash blonde hair allowed to grow long, cut in a fringe. He looked as if butter would not melt in his mouth, but was very full of mischief. The youngest was my darling. Ruth aged two. Very shy, gentle like Mutti. She would peep out, her blonde curly hair a fringe, at a world completely alien to her. As long as we were together all was well with her world. Apart from any of us, especially from me, she was a lost soul. These four were known as Kerry's children and were my pride and joy. Loved beyond words, looked after and protected to the best of my ability. We were lucky, we at least were a family. Our love for one another was like a well. The more love we gave, the more there was to give.

We had never before been parted. Now we had no choice. As always we did as we were told. The sexes even at this early age were segregated. Boys slept on the first floor, we girls on the second. Rows of beds ran either side of the long room. Also on this floor were the bathrooms and toilets. This was the first time I encountered showers. I was fascinated by them and enjoyed the feel of water all over my skin.

Life in the orphanage was routine. Each child knew its duties and carried them out. Work was a necessity. Meals to be cooked, floors to be polished, smaller children to be looked after. The latter was no hardship for me. There was no talking, no noise of any description, just silence. A strange life for children. We did not talk, we whispered; did not run, walked sedately. All very unchildlike.

We existed in this cold house. When one reads of orphanages in the here and now, one thinks of places like Dr. Barnardo's, large airy houses with happy children living in an atmosphere of affection if not love. In my time at the Orphanage there was neither affection nor love from the people who looked after us. Even that comment is incorrect; no one looked after us, we, looked after ourselves. No non-Jewish person would go into a Jewish orphanage to clean, cook or do the million and one things it takes to look after forty or so children. It was the girls who did the housework.

The boys were allowed to go to a small Jewish school. Only for a while. It was important for them to continue to learn Hebrew as well as normal subjects. Boys become Barmitzvah at thirteen. In the Jewish religion, this means coming of age. (How was I to know my boys would never reach this age.) Studying was the norm for all Jewish boys. For us girls, it did not matter. As long as we could read Hebrew, which I still can, other duties came first. We girls were much too busy working to keep the place clean, cook the meals, wash the clothes and polish anything that did not move. The Superintendent was very fussy and about everything that could be polished had to be.

The actual orphanage was very large. Set in many acres of fields and a playing field for football or whatever children with time on their hands wanted to play outside, though this became a rarity, going outside being too hazardous. Who knew when the Hitler Youths would come and harass any of us were we in the open. There was no room to play in the house. Places to eat, sleep, bathe and the schoolrooms, but no place to relax and just be a child.

To gain entry to the orphanage you rang a bell at the very

37

large forbidding gates. Visitors were rare, but there were special occasions early in our time at the orphanage when people came. I can remember Passover. So very different from what we had known at home with Opa. The people who came to the Seder were strangers to us. It became a place to congregate and be together. But all this was before 1938. So much changed after that time. Unwelcome visitors came only too often. These would ring the bell furiously, shouting their demands to enter at the top of their voices and of course there was no way to keep them out.

The large gates, through which we were never allowed to leave except on some special occasion, were no deterrent to the Hitler Youths who roamed the streets looking for trouble. There was a day of horror, never to be forgotten. They, the Hitler Youth, decided that the older children in the orphanage should learn a lesson. They came to the gates demanding they be opened. The Superintendent had no choice but to give in to this mob. They came looking for us older children; the eldest might have been twelve or thirteen. I was only about eight at the time, so was to them old enough for what they had in mind. In Kassel most of the people lived in apartments. Houses were only on the outskirts of the town. Two doors from the orphanage there was a tall house about four stories high. The Hitler Youths dragged a poor old man to the top window. They had stripped him naked. I could see the confusion on his face. He was one of the many scholars who had no idea what went on outside his room. His life had been spent in this one room, which was his world. Here he studied the Hebrew scriptures. I can only imagine the shock he felt at the intrusion of this gang of Hitler Youths. To be suddenly attacked, stripped and held out of the window. All we below could see was this poor old naked man with his long white beard and a look of astonishment on his face. Suddenly the youths let him fall. We watched in horror as he hurtled through the air, plummeted like a stone and landed at our feet. Shall never forget the strange sound of his fall and the crack as his head hit the pavement. His skull split open and there almost at our feet, blood and brains surrounded what was once a human being, one who would not have hurt a soul. As long as I live I shall never forget the sight or the sound of this horror. I have rarely spoken of this incident. Perhaps had I confronted this horror and spoken of it more often, it might not have become a recurring nightmare, one of many that haunted me and turned me into an insomniac.

Not all the children were orphans; we of course had Papa and Mutti, even if we were parted from them. The fact that we knew they existed was what made life in this cold unhappy place bearable. Some Sundays Rolf and I would be allowed to visit Mutti in the camp. We walked five miles each way; we were aged seven and eight and thought nothing of walking such a distance. To see Mutti we would have walked on our knees. Mutti again was pregnant and had Ludwig, the baby, always hanging on her skirts; he was only eighteen months old. I shall never know how she coped. I remember how she thanked God for the young men in the camp. They of course were the homosexuals, a word I did not know then – but I know that I will be forever grateful to them for their kindness and help to my mother. I never knew where the food to feed her and Ludwig came from. She must have gone through hell. It was winter and to go to the toilet she would have had to queue with many others. To have water, again she had to queue; though I believe the young men did this for her. It seemed we had only just arrived to see her, when it was time to return. These trips I believe were all that kept us going. Seeing Mutti, even for such a short time, was our idea of heaven. We regretted being unable to help her, but we were children, what could we do. My job was to be with my younger children and do the best I could for them..

Then came my testing time. Early 1938, Hitler had again sent forth one more of his decrees. This time, it was to stop Jews from buying food in a German store. We were only allowed to shop in the one Jewish shop. I cannot in all honesty remember how many children were in the orphanage, I am sure not less than fifty. How would it be possible to feed that many mouths from one small shop? The answer was it was impossible. My children, though no angels, never cried unless there was a very good reason. This they now had. They were hungry. All the other children were hungry too. How can you fill stomachs with sour milk sprinkled with sugar? My concern was very selfish. My children were the only ones who mattered to me. I tolerated their cries for a little longer then I visited the Superintendent's office which was only visited when a child had been naughty or did something wrong. My heart, pounding like a hammer, I knocked and was told to enter. The surprise on this lady's face plus the look of disapproval was enough to make me want to run away. I had a job to do and do it I must. All we children except Rolf, my one-year younger brother, were blonde with blue eyes. Rolf was darker and had brown eyes. Because I had long blonde plaits and looked more German than some of the children on the street, I thought my plan would work and proceeded to ask a very shocked lady for money. I told her I wanted to go shopping in the town taking Rolf with me. Her first stupid question was 'why?' 'My children are hungry.' Thought that was quite enough information. She continued to look at me. After what seemed like hours, she consented and gave me money. Day after day Rolf and I went food shopping. We had enough sense not to go to the same shops too often. No children crying – it was wonderful. Our expeditions lasted perhaps for two months. Then one day I had the feeling that we were being followed, but took no notice. My mistake. We arrived at the gates to find a gang of Hitler Youths. Yes, they had been following us. They took our basket from us and proceeded to beat us both until we were almost unconscious, and threatened us with dire warnings as to what would happen if they caught us again. They threw us into the grounds of the home with the older children and the Superintendent carried us into the house and put us to bed. Never one to leave well enough alone, the dear lady reiterated the Youths' warning. Thinking this would deter me from thoughts of future shopping expeditions. This lady did not know me at all. My stubbornness, my almost suicidal care for my children. Had I explained she would not have understood. She knew nothing of the love I had for them. She seemed to know nothing of love. My whole life had no value except to look after and care for my children. Again and again I had to listen to them crying with hunger. My bruises had healed and once again I went to the office. 'Now what do you want, have you learned nothing from your beating.' 'Yes,' I replied, 'my children are hungry and I want to go shopping.' I thought she was going to strike me there and then. 'I cannot be responsible for a repeat performance,' she said. 'If you do not give me money I will go and steal it,' I replied. She looked in my eyes and said she believed I would do what I had threatened. Little did she know I had no more idea how to steal money than I knew how to fly to the moon. I had stolen apples off trees. That was all I knew of stealing. Once again she reluctantly gave me money. I found Rolf and we went shopping. This time we left by the bottom meadow which we, in our ignorance, thought was unknown. Here I should add some more explanation about the Hitler Youths. They stood on street corners dressed in fancy uniforms just waiting for trouble, mainly Jewish trouble. They would beat up any Jew they saw, be it man, woman or child, and nobody would interfere or say them nay. They were a law unto themselves. We visited shops where we thought we had not been seen before, which was difficult as we had to walk miles returning with a heavy basket. We went out each day as before. Unfortunately our luck did not last. The Hitler Youths continued to follow us. When they found we had not learned our lesson, they brought the Gestapo to wait for us at the little gate. The Gestapo took us to their headquarters where they beat us with truncheons. An eight and nine year old, small for our age, but they did not care. Age did not matter. We were Jews and had ignored a decree of their 'God' Hitler. They took us back and threw us into the grounds of the orphanage. We were put to bed. And a doctor was called. (This beating was so dreadful that I was left with two faulty kidneys. In later years these cost me two miscarriages and scars I still carry on my body.)

Life went on pretty much as usual. I had to listen to my children crying because they were hungry, but could do nothing about it. To say I was frustrated at my inability to help them is an understatement. By this time I needed them as much as they needed me, our love for one another was what kept us going.

I must have been born under a very malevolent star. Anything that could go wrong had to go wrong with me. I woke one morning with raging toothache. I had never been to a dentist in my life nor ever had toothache. This pain went on day after day until it became unbearable, even the Superintendent was worried. She contacted dentist after dentist, but we were Jews. No one cared if Jews suffered, we were the non-human. Eventually to her amazement, she found a dentist who would see me. She went with me for protection, though I have no idea what she thought she could do. We were shown into a white tiled room and made to sit in an odd chair. The dentist came in. I started to shake and cry. Me cry, no one had ever seen this before. How I feared this monster who stood in front of me. This was no man who would make me feel better. He wore a white coat, as did a doctor, but could no one see his jackboots. He held me down with his knee in my stomach. In his hand he held a strange, terrifying, noisy, pointed needle. He did not look for the tooth that gave me so much pain; he just drilled and drilled until I fainted. He had drilled right through to my jaw. When I came round he smiled the smile of a monster and said 'This is the way I like to see Dirty Jews, with their blood running over my boots'. I will never forget that excuse for a man, nor the smile of enjoyment and pleasure on his face. Despite the beatings I had endured, firstly from children, then Hitler Youth and then the beatings with truncheons from the Gestapo, I still had not really taken in the satanic menace of the Nazis. But this incident, more than all that had gone before, brought home to me the fear and horror of this regime. I was only nine years old, but suddenly I knew the bestiality in this world where it was a crime to be a Jew. This was a world I had no choice but live in. To me the most important thing was to keep my children safe.

Kristallnacht

18th NOVEMBER 1938. Never to be forgotten. During the day we had listened in fear to the sound of breaking glass, shouting and noises we could not identify. As evening came, we saw from the upstairs windows, fire in the sky, the whole town seemed to be lit up. When we saw the direction of the fires, we realised that both our synagogues were alight. Still the shouting and singing went on. This of course was Kristallnacht. In English the night of broken glass. We cried, I think more in frustration at this wanton destruction and the fact that there was nothing we could do. Suddenly we were called downstairs. The Superintendent thought we had seen enough. We had not been downstairs very long when a timid knock came at the door which I was the one to answer. On the doorstep were two very old men, each carrying a Torah, which is the most holy thing and belonged in the ark of the synagogue. I had no idea how these two very old men had managed to get to us. They did not want to come in and endanger us children, but wanted us to hide the Torahs. They did not think an orphanage would be searched. Against the wishes of the Superintendent, we children carried the Torahs with great reverence and hid them in an airing cupboard. To this day I do not know what happened to them.

Now it was our turn, we lived in a Jewish house and therefore one ready to be burnt. They threw bottles filled with petrol, which they lit. Of course, I did not at the time know what these were. But learnt many years later that they were called Molotov cocktails. There was complete chaos. We older children took the little ones upstairs out of harm's way. The downstairs of the house was well alight, so we found buckets, saucepans to carry the water. We worked like adults. We were not children. These things could not happen to children. We worked all night putting out small fires. Had they been left, they would have burnt down the orphanage. After all, this was the only home we knew and it was up to us to see to its safety. We worked throughout the night and eventually managed to put the fire out. We looked like chimney sweeps, but our tasks were not finished. Now came the time to clear up the mess the fire and water had made. A very tired and weary brigade of children, beyond tiredness really, we cleaned and swept, until the place looked almost as before. Admittedly, there was no shine on floors or doors, but we had beaten the fire.

Exhausted as we were, there was still no time to relax. First we had to clean ourselves up. This time no one cared whether girls and boys were segregated. We all went under the showers, line after line of weary but triumphant children. Then we had to see to the little ones. They had not had anything to eat or drink during the previous evening or in the morning. The kitchen was manned by a troupe of children, heating milk and finding what we could to feed our little ones. Only after they were fed could we think of ourselves. We truly could do no more. Thankfully we went to our beds. I am sure we all slept the sleep of the dead.

We came from our beds at last to hear the Superintendent say how proud she was of us all. I can remember how strange this seemed. We had not considered what we had done was out of the ordinary. This was our home so of course we had defended it in the only way we could. On reflection, you could say now that we really were not children, we had suffered too much. We were small adults and thought and worked as such. That night will never be forgotten by anyone. It was a turning point. We Jews had been harried, beaten, spat on and generally ill-treated before Kristallnacht. Now there was no holding the bullies. Beatings, looting and general mayhem were even more the order of the day. No Jew ventured out of doors unless forced to. All male adults, and this included older boys, were rounded up and sent to concentration camps. I thanked God that my children were all younger than me, I was nine and would be ten in January. If possible, life became harder after Kristallnacht. Food, as always, was in short supply. What was different was the fear that had infected all the children. Without us knowing, it had crept upon us when dealing with the fire. A night of such terror had to leave its mark.

The Journey to Wales

I HAVE ALWAYS had an aversion to having my photograph taken. This time I had no choice. A photographer came to the home and took photographs of all us children. Not a scary thing in itself, but as always no reason was given. Someone said 'Smile' and we did as we were told and smiled. It was an effort, we really had nothing to smile about. Life went back to its normal grind, washing, cleaning, and looking after my children. The latter was no hardship. My children, Rolf, Heinz, Sally and the youngest, my beautiful sister Ruth, had become my life. The love that flowed between us made up for a lot of hardships and other miseries, the main one being that we were no longer allowed out of the Orphanage to see Mutti; had not seen her since Kristallnacht. With no way to contact her or for her to contact us, this was very hard to bear.

Time went by, no way to count the days or months, each day like the next. One morning the Superintendent sent for me. This was serious. No one was sent for unless they had done something wrong. I could think of nothing. Very slowly I went down to the hall, clinging to the banister which like everything else gleamed from all the polishing. When I walked the length of this enormous hall, I saw someone sitting on a chair by the office. As I came closer, this someone stood up. I could not believe my eyes. Was this my handsome Papa with his blonde curly hair, which after his strength and looks was the first thing that one noticed? How could this skeleton with a shaved head possibly be him? He held out his arms and hugged me. This was not a normal occurrence; he could see the shock I had received. After that, each day he came and together we would visit office after office. Papers were signed. Yet never was any of this explained to me. What was it about? Why would no one tell me? Days passed still without explanation. I did what I was told. The children asked why? What? Where? But I had no answer for them.

One day a car pulled up outside the orphanage. Papa and

Mutti and a now walking Ludwig sat in the car whilst I was hurried out of the house to join them. There was no time to say 'goodbye' to my children, and I had not been told where I was going. We arrived at the station. What an enormous place. I had never seen either a station or a train. What were we doing there? Suddenly I was hugged and kissed by Mutti and Papa who picked me up, lifted me onto this iron monster and shut the doors. Despite all my tears, there was a heavy door and windows between us and there was nothing I could do. All my tears were of no avail.

It would have made a little sense had I been told what to expect, but knowing nothing but panic as the train started to move, the scene that is for ever in my mind is seeing Papa and Mutti growing smaller and smaller as the train moved further away. This was the last time I saw Mutti and the rest of my children. I had not even been able to say goodbye to them. It was a dreadful thing to do, to rip a ten-year-old child from her family without explanation.

Here I think I must explain what had happened. The photographs that were taken in the Orphanage had been sent all over the world, much as a catalogue, from which to choose a child. Some thousands of children had been chosen to go to America, Canada, Australia, wherever the photographs ended up. The larger countries took a few thousand children, Canada closed its doors completely. The United States took some thousands. Great Britain, the smallest country, took 10,000 children between 1938 and 1939. Not all stayed in Britain. Some went to Israel; others, if they had relations in other countries, went to join them. Relations they had never even seen. My photograph came to a small town in South Wales called Swansea and to an elderly couple, he seventy and she fifty. They had never had children and wanted someone to look after them in their old age. But more of that later.

As the train pulled away, I was terrified. What was happening? Why was I on this strange contraption? Where was it taking me? Why was I having to leave Mutti and Papa? I did not want to go away from them. I did not want to be alone, it was not fair. There was nothing I could do about it. How was it that my parents were getting smaller and smaller? Had I done something wrong and was it my punishment to be sent away? Nothing made sense except this awful loneliness. Why could I not have stayed with Rolf, Heinz, Bubbi and Ruth? What would they do without me? How could I live without them? Questions and more questions, but no answers.

All I knew was a new loneliness. I had never been without my family and they had never been without me. My mind was going round in circles. Why were Mutti and Papa getting smaller? I could hardly see them and yet they stayed in my eyes. I was not to know that this was a permanent state that I was to live with throughout my life. The here and now was impossible to contemplate, so it seems my mind switched off. I have no memory of the rest of that journey. Was I alone? Were there other children with me? Who knows? I do not.

I have no recollection of how long the journey took. The next thing to frighten me was when the train stopped at Hamburg. In all my life, I had never seen water larger than the village pond, and thought that was large. Suddenly I was confronted with this enormous amount of water and could not take it in. Where did all this water come from and where was it going? Then I saw a very large house on this water. How big it was. How could it stay on the water? Again questions and questions, but never an answer. We were herded on to a narrow plank of wood and told to cross it into the big house. It was very scary. We had never had picture books so I had never seen the sea and certainly not so much water. I heard someone call this house a ship, so what was a ship, no different from a funny shaped house. Eventually all the children, I had not realised that we were so many, it never even occurred to me that I was part of this group, were ushered on to the ship.

I have very little memory of this part of the journey but some things remain. There were children present of all ages, all shapes, all sizes and they were as bewildered as I was. Suddenly a lady came to me holding a very small girl, perhaps three or four. The child couldn't stop crying. I had dealt with babies and small children all my life, but how did these people know that? I took the child in my arms. How good that felt, I could pretend it was my Ruth. So I cuddled her and rocked her till she stopped crying. I held on to the child not wanting anyone to take her from me, after all, this little mite filled my empty arms. I must have slept for it was a while before I realised that the ship had stopped moving. The lady who had given me the small child, came and told me I had to give the little mite back. My arms were empty again. I so wanted to cry, but what was the use.

Soon we were herded together again but this time off the ship. What was so different? I was still alone despite all the children around me. Yet something was different. No idea what it could be. Then I realised what it was. There was no feeling of fear, people were shouting and children crying, but not from the fear we had known in Germany. It was a strange thing for a ten-year-old child to work out. My mind was working, but in slow motion. I could still see my parents getting smaller, my arms still ached for my brothers and sisters. All those years we had never been parted. Now I was alone in a very large crowd of children and the pain was that they were not my children, they were strangers, and even the little girl I had nursed was gone. For the first time I knew what loneliness was. It was more than just being alone, for how could I be alone with all these children around me? It was an emptiness that hurt like a pain and would not ease. I did not know then that it would never ease. That it was to be with me all my life. Circumstances had taken me away from my parents and my children and I could do nothing about it.

We were cared for by strangers. On the train, each seat had a little box on it. Being very polite children, not one of us thought of opening their box until a lady came and told us we could open this little treasure chest. In the box, I can see it now, there was an apple, a round orange thing, a funny shaped yellow thing which had to be fruit, for the apple I knew was fruit, and some sweets. I remembered all the apples I had sneaked out from behind the wire on the Kassel road. So I knew about apples, pears, peaches that grew against walls and cherries we had climbed trees for. But these two strange fruits I had never seen before. Were the sweets in the box Kosher? A strange thought from a child who had been starving. As the train went along, I decided to try the yellow thing. It tasted dreadful. As I was eating it, a lady came into the compartment. There were many ladies going along the corridors. The one that came into us looked at me strangely and said, 'Child you have to peel the banana, it cannot be eaten with peel on'. When she had peeled the thing called a banana, I tried eating it more to please her than because I wanted to eat this dreadful tasting fruit. I suppose it was because I still had the taste of the peel in my mouth that it tasted so bad. The lady went on her way and to take the taste of bitterness from my mouth, I started to eat what she had called an orange. Oh dear, I had not been told that this too had to be peeled. Again a dreadful taste so I gave up eating fruit.

The train journey seemed to go on forever. I found it impossible to talk to the other children. I had never had trouble communicating with the other children in the orphanage. This, of course, was different. These children were strangers, and I think I was still in shock. I only had to think of Mutti and Papa and they were still there in front of my eyes, getting smaller and smaller. Scenery meant nothing to me so I investigated my very small case. Inside were a change of underclothes, a pair of knickers, pair of socks, a vest, hanky and little more. There at the bottom lay my great treasure, a photograph of all my family, taken whilst we were still in our old, lovely house. This picture must have been taken early in 1937 for Ludwig had just been born and was in Mutti's arms. It could not be dated by the clothes we wore. They were our best and had been for sometime. I wore a blue velvet dress which can be seen in every photograph ever taken of me; in the picture that was taken in the orphanage, on my Exit Visa and now here I was travelling in the same dress, despite it being the end of June 1939. I must have worn it in all seasons, for I had no other. I held and kissed that photograph, a last reminder of my family and my most treasured possession.

After what seemed an everlasting journey, we arrived in London and went up the steps of a large building. All of us wore huge labels with our names in big letters. My luck was out once again. Everything was done with precision and we were seated alphabetically. My surname being Wertheim, my seat was way up in the top of the building. As names were called, each child walked down these steps and was met and introduced to a perfect stranger. There were a few exceptions, the ones met by members of their family, perhaps distant, but they were family, these were the lucky few. After what seemed a very long time, my name was called. It seemed miles down those many steps. At the bottom stood a very old man. He looked eight foot tall. He was in fact over six foot, but to a child, a very small ten year old, he seemed enormous. I was told his name; he already knew mine. Like all well brought up children, I curtsied, for girls did this, just as boys bowed to their elders. He took my hand and we went outside into a car; this was a taxi of course. Soon there was another station and another train. I had by now discovered to my horror that we had no common language. He could not speak German and I could not speak a word of English. As we waited for our train, I saw in the window of a little shop on the platform, some peaches. I kept looking at them, would not point, this was very bad manners, if I knew nothing else, good manners were automatic. So I stood and looked at these peaches, till my tall companion suddenly realised what I wanted. He went into the little shop and came out with a big bag of peaches. He gave them to me and when I took them, I could almost hear his sigh of relief.

Our train came and we had a compartment all to ourselves. In 1939 it took about six hours from London to Swansea, a time that was spent in total silence for we had no common language. He did try some strange language, in which there were a few German words, but it meant nothing. I later discovered he had been speaking Yiddish, a mixture of Russian, Polish and German, a language Jewish people use to make themselves understood when they have no common language. I spoke only

German, so this was no use. I forgot to say that he had been introduced as Herr Feigenbaum. What a journey. I was not sure if I was sorrier for myself or this man, he tried so hard to put me at ease. The only time he even looked happy was when I ate the peaches and he took out his handkerchief and wiped my chin. I, so wanting to please him, insisted that he too ate a peach, then I too could wipe his chin. Thus we passed a very very long journey. Until, at last we arrived at our destination, Swansea.

Part Two
Wales

New Parents

WHAT WAS SWANSEA? As we entered the train in London, I heard a man who went up and down outside, shouting Swansea, Swansea. I had no idea what he was saying, but I was struck by the word and the funny voice he had. When our long journey ended, there was another man shouting Swansea. He sounded very different. So again, what was Swansea?

My dear man took my hand and my little box, then helped me down the steps of the train. I was frightened; there were so many people. They surrounded me and spoke in a language that made no sense to me. A big man with a large, pretty chain about his neck took my hand and shook it. This of course made me curtsy as I had been taught. I looked about to see my nice man and found he had been joined by a little lady. She too was old, not as old as the tall man, but as old as Oma was when I had last seen her. She held out her hand and took mine. Why had she done that and who was she? I was getting more and more confused. Suddenly a much younger man came from the back of the crowd of people, took my hand and spoke to me in German. The relief was wonderful, but very short-lived. He told me that the nice man I had been travelling with was my Papa and the little lady was my Mutti. This really was more than I could take. I screamed and cried, no way were they my parents, had I not left them not so long ago and were they not still in my eyes. These two new people could not be my parents; they were old, old as Opa and Oma. There was noise and consternation. Why was this strange child making such a fuss, screaming and crying? They had not understood what the man had told me as he and I had been speaking German.

From now on, I will have to refer to them, the nice man and the lady, as my mother and father for convenience sake. At this stage, of course, I could not speak English, so even these words had no meaning. The couple took me by the hand, we left the station and a car took us to their home, a very tall house in the centre of town. Mother took me upstairs to take off my cloak, an article of clothing I had received in one of the parcels of Erika's old clothes many years ago. I had always loved wearing it, for I could pull it around myself and hide from the world. I had never allowed myself to cry in front of other children. This cloak was my escape. Was the pretty room I found myself in just for me? I had never had a whole room to myself before and would have given anything to have Ruth share it with me. Felt so alone and lonely. I followed mother to the bathroom to wash my hands, then downstairs to the dining room. Waiting at the table was father, a man I grew to love. I know he loved me, but was never allowed to show it, my new mother would not permit it.

It is time to tell more about these two people who had, as they thought, given me a home. They didn't know I would have preferred to be at the orphanage with my children. Father was a very tall, gentle man with a heart as big as a house. Unfortunately, as I have said, he was not allowed to show his gentleness and sweetness. As far as mother was concerned he was her property and must only feel for her. He was seventy years old, self educated and well educated. He had a wonderful library, always under lock and key. He so loved his books. He had come from Russia many years ago and had taught himself excellent English. He was a staunch Labour follower and very well thought of by all who knew him. This is just a nutshell of a description of a wonderful man. He had a bald head, smiley eyes and was loving and tender. Not a handsome man but, from the start, when I looked into his eyes I knew I could trust this dear man with my life.

Mother was a very different person. She was fifty years old, had never had any children and did not really want any for she was far too selfish to share her very pleasant and easy life with anyone. She and father had been married twenty years. Father had always spoiled her and there was no way she would let anyone change this state of affairs. She was one of the most selfish people I have ever met. Her heart was made of pure ice. There was no kindness or affection in her. She came first, last and all the time. I believe it was her idea to bring me to Britain for her own selfish ends. Let me explain. This was a woman who had never worked. She had always had a maid to do her house-work. The only work she did was cook. To give the devil her due, she was a wonderful cook.

Father had a business. Making accessories for ladies clothes. He made a very good living and mother had no trouble spend-ing the money he had worked for. She went to the cinema across the road from the house at least twice or three times a week. All other days were taken up with playing Bridge. There were many other ladies of leisure of her acquaintance who had nothing better to do than play cards. How I came to hate this. She was short, rather tubby but with quite a pretty face and grey wavy hair. She always looked smart and spent a small fortune on clothes. She looked very stiff. At the time, I did not realise that she wore a corset. A strange contraption which I only saw by accident. There was no way she would allow anyone to see this except by accident. It was a wide piece of hard material, made harder by whalebones which made the garment stand up by itself. I had never seen such a thing and had no idea what it was for. When I knew mother better and I saw the way she stood, only then did this garment make some sense. I could never work out why anyone would wear something so uncomfortable. Mother of course was vain to the nth degree.

The house was always spotless. Phyllis, her maid, worked very hard to keep it this way. Nothing was ever out of place. The house was always ready for entertaining her Bridge friends. Most of whom were elderly unmarried ladies with nothing to do with their time. With her, Bridge had become a religion and how I came to hate it. It had been her idea to foster me, planning for me to look after father and her in their old age.

That first time, we came into the dining room to a heavily laden table with food I could not recognise. Just so much food. All I could think about was my children. They were hungry and here was food enough for all in the Orphanage. The sight of so much food made me feel very ill. Mother was watching me and could not understand why I would not eat. Even had I spoken English, she would not have understood. Food in this quantity was unbelievable and nothing on the table was familiar. As hard as I tried, there was no way I could even put out my hand to pick up any of it. All I could think about was that all this food would have been sufficient to feed not only my children, but most of the children in the Orphanage. This thought alone made me want to cry once again. Had I seen anything I could recognise, I would have eaten, if only to please this lady I now had to call mother. When I looked for something, anything that I could find familiar, I saw bread but even this was wrong. In Germany, bread was black, on this table it was white. Had mother had any understanding of children, she had only to look at my exhausted face to realise how very tired and weary I was. Unfortunately, she had no such understanding. Out of sheer frustration, she pointed me to the stairs and my bedroom. I am sure she thought it some sort of punishment, but this was the very relief for which I had waited. I washed and got into the large bed. After so much physical and emotional weariness, I was sure I would be able to sleep. But sleep was long in coming. Sounds strange to say that I was not a weeping child, when I wrote not long ago about hysterics. Normally I had learned to take life as it came and make the best of it. Now everything unravelled, I wanted my children, my Ruth in my arms but my arms were empty and my heart full of pain. Eventually I must have slept.

Next morning I awoke completely bewildered. Where was I? Where was Ruth? Each morning in the Orphanage the moment she woke up, she came to my bed. Now I looked about me and saw a strange room. Then I remembered the day before. What was I expected to do? Be up and about? I needed to go to the toilet, what if there was anyone in there, what then? Decided the bathroom was a necessity, so the choice was made. Washed, went back to my room which I had somehow accepted was my room now. I dressed and went downstairs. Found the dining room and again a table laid. This time not as laden as the day before. Mother must have realised something was wrong. She came into the room bearing a teapot. Here again I was confused. In the

Orphanage, we drank nothing but milk and water; coffee was only for grownups. I looked at the pot and shook my head. In retrospect, to some extent I feel sorry for her, she could do nothing right for she knew nothing about children. The big pot was in her right hand and in the left was another pot. This she held out to me. What a relief, it was filled with milk and I nodded my head. She too was relieved and we sat down at the table. Father had arrived by this time and smiled at me, more than mother had done. He was served first, then the performance started again. What could I eat? By this time I could not have cared less, anything to take the frown off this lady's face. She offered me what looked like burned bread, toast of course, and butter which I knew. Then marmalade. I was once again stumped. Out of desperation I took some. It was delicious and, at my pleasure, she smiled for the first time.

Thus started the first morning, if it had only continued as it started all would have been as well as it could be, but this lady had ideas of her own. The first one was the worst. She had decided that she did not like my plaits, so she took me to a hairdresser and had her cut them off. I cried as if my heart would burst, and so I thought it would. I looked in the mirror and found a stranger looking at me, but there was nothing I could do, the deed had been done. She did, however, have the cut hair packed to be taken home. She found an empty chocolate box and packed my pride and joy, the hair that had saved my life so often. She put it into this box and gave it to me, as if she was doing me a great favour. I could not speak a word, had no language to make myself understood to them, and even if I had been able to speak English, would not have said a word. I had been well trained in the orphanage, where one does not question what an adult says or does. When we returned home father took one look and started to shake his head and spoke to mother very sharply. It was too late. This was not to be the end of the things she did not like about me.

I have explained that well brought up German children bow if a boy and curtsy when a girl. This was as natural as breathing. Mother did not approve. Each time I curtsied, she would hit me at the back of my knee to make me stop. Eventually, though thinking her very rude, I got the message. I didn't feel right about this 'discourtesy' for a very long time. Disaster number three: she did not like my name, Kerry. I had always been called this and had no idea I had another name. She insisted on calling me Ellen. I had never heard this name before and each time she called Ellen I did not answer. Who was this Ellen? I was Kerry, a name she never used.

The days passed, not one day went by without some hassle or other, the 'Ellen' business the worst. There was no one to tell me what I was doing wrong or how to please her. I had put up with having my hair cut. Had learned not to curtsy. What more could I do? Still she was always cross. It seemed there was nothing that I could do that pleased her no matter how hard I tried. The number of things of which she disapproved was endless. When she realised I had only one change of underclothes and one dress, we had to go out to buy me clothes. I believe she actually liked doing this. Again her sense of charity was reinforced.

Each day I did what I thought was expected of me, recognised some of the signs which told me what meant Yes and No. Anyone can nod or shake their head; only this made sense. If I was expected to eat, I was pointed to a chair at the table. Bed was easy, and my only escape from mother.

Mother never did housework and left it all to Phyllis who had a boyfriend called Dave. She was very beautiful, both inside and outside. Dave was a miner and in his spare time a boxer. He had a funny face, his nose was spread all across it, but when he smiled he was handsome. He was as beautiful in his way as my Phyllis was in hers. These two people showed me affection in many small and important ways. They loved this strange child even though we could not communicate. When mother was not around, Phyllis would hug and kiss me, making loving noises to try and take away the pain she could see on my face. Dave was never allowed into the house, so Phyllis and I met him in the garden out of sight of mother. These two wonderful people helped save my life and my sanity, how I loved them both and will never forget them.

Father's business included a workshop where all the buttons were made, edging put on hems and other sorts of finishes done to complete the making of dresses. Here he employed four girls. I cannot remember their names or ages, but am sure they must have been in their late teens or perhaps a little older. At ten everyone seems old. These delightful girls took me to their hearts. Whenever mother started shouting, she could be heard throughout the house. As soon as I could get away from her I would immediately make for the workshop. There the door was always open to receive me and I could hide and feel safe. So many things these wonderful girls did for me. Mother thought I had no need for pocket money. I, of course, did not even know what this was. Father insisted when I started school that I must have some money to spend. This caused a commotion. Mother insisted that there was no need. There were always sweets and chocolates in the house, she was very partial to chocolates. This insensitive woman could not understand that she had made it impossible for me to ask her for anything, there was no way I would be the cause of an argument. The girls were paid on a Friday. I do not think their wages were all that much but what they had they were more than willing to share. In the workshop there stood a large round mirror on a stand. Each Friday each girl would put a half penny under the stand thus making sure that I had pocket money. Another great treat were their lunch times. Around the corner from our house stood a very well known fish-and-chip shop called 'The Windsor'. Living in a Kosher Jewish family, it was forbidden to eat anything that was not cooked at home. It never occurred to me that these tasty chips which the girls bought for their lunch and shared with me were cooked in lard. Not that I would have known what lard was. I had always known that anything to do with a pig was taboo, how was I to know that the chips were forbidden food for me. I just enjoyed them. I cannot praise these wonderful girls too much. We had no common language yet they loved and understood me without words.

New Life

WEEKS PASSED; mother thought it high time for me to go to school. I knew Yes and No, but no other word of English. Day one at Terrace Road School and mother took me to see the head-mistress, Miss Davies. She looked very stern so I did not know what to expect. Anything was better than hanging about the house with nothing to do. Once mother had left, Miss Davies took me into a class of many children, all about my age. She introduced me to the teacher in charge, and left me there. It was such luck to meet her. Miss Tucker was the most patient person I had ever met. We could not speak one another's language, but that did not seem to matter. There is no way I can explain how her patience affected me, suffice it to say that in a very short time I was speaking a very garbled English. At last I could make myself understood. What a relief. At last I knew who Ellen was. Miss Tucker explained to me that my name was Ellen and not Kerry. It was very difficult to understand why I had to change names, but I had been introduced to the school as Ellen. Not long after I had managed to learn some English, I was called to the Headmistress's office and told I must learn Welsh. Truly, after that, I did try, but without much success. Miss Davies realised it was too much to ask of a child just learn-ing to speak another language. So I concentrated on English. A language I came to love.

By now it must have been the end of July. War was very much in the air. I found it difficult to understand why little boys followed me to school and threw stones at me and called me Nazi. How could they do such a thing? This was Britain and people did not do things like stone throwing and name calling here. When Miss Davies heard about it, she asked two girls who lived near our house to accompany me to school. Then she visited the Boys school; I gather she had harsh words to say to the Headmaster about his rotten boys. Never one to mince words Miss Davies. The harassment soon stopped, never to be repeated.

Terrace Road school was situated a long way from

Northampton Place where I lived. The journey was uphill all the way. First a little hill, then what seemed like hundreds of steps then yet another hill before we reached the school. The view from the top over Swansea, the Bay and all the way to Mumbles Head in one direction and Port Talbot in the other was wonderful. The trip had to be made four times a day. Twice up and twice down, because I went home for lunch. In those days there were no school lunches, but even if there had been I would not have been allowed to eat anywhere except home. When you are ten or eleven such long treks mean nothing. Looking back, they just meant being out of the house a bit longer. In winter the treks were not much fun. The hills and the steps were icy. But I was always reminded of the tobogganing with my brothers and sister. They were never far from my mind, my heart hurt constantly with my need for them.

I did not hear anything from Mutti until August. A postcard arrived telling me I had a new sister named Zilla. Then silence, not another word. One day, it must have been the end of August, I received a postcard from the Isle of Wight. It was difficult to believe what I read. It came from Papa; he had escaped from Germany and had come to Britain where he was treated as an 'Enemy Alien' and interned. It was very difficult to understand. I was too young to make sense of what had happened. I learned many, many years later, Papa had decided he could do nothing for Mutti or the children by returning to Dachau. So he decided there and then he would get to Britain and somehow he did. We exchanged cards; Papa never did like writing letters.

As I write this, a strange memory comes to mind. Oma Wertheim and all the uncles and of course Erika, Papa's younger sister, only two years older than me, had all emigrated to America in 1937. I do not remember nor saw the letter Papa wrote to her at the time, only remember his rage at the letter he had in return. He had begged, a very hard thing for this man to do, asking Oma Wertheim to send a letter to the authorities telling them she would stand surety for all of us, if we would be allowed to go to America. I can still see the look on his face as he read the letter, it was truly frightening. He gave the letter to both Mutti and to me to read saying, 'I have no mother, she is dead to me and to all of us.' The letter told Papa that she would not, not could not, write such a letter. I cannot remember what excuses she used. It was the 'would not' that hurt so much. After that, I never heard Oma's name mentioned.

But now Papa was in the Isle of Wight. Some months passed. Then a card arrived telling me that he was coming to Swansea to see me. It was a strange visit. Papa and I spoke German, mother and father did not understand and my English was so little that there was no way I could translate. Seeing Papa again was a gift from heaven.

Before Papa came to see me for the first time, the only time I spent with father was on Sundays when in his bowler hat and smart suit he would take me for a walk. The part of Swansea he was most fond of was the Guildhall, a new building which had been built in 1936. I was not really interested in the building itself but loved to go a little further where we could see the sea and play on the beach. I had come to love the sea. Sunday mornings were the only time I was given this treat. Mother did not know about it; she would not have approved. Father was very proud of our beach and all the surrounding bays. This was what he wanted Papa to see when he came. So we went on a picnic in Uncle and Auntie Wolf's car. Papa was duly impressed and kept telling me how lucky I was. I did not tell him of all the misery I had to bear. I wanted the two days he was with me to be perfect. Mother of course was a very different person in public. She pretended to care for me – all sham. The days soon passed and Papa had to return to his unit. He had been put in the Pioneer Corps. His visit was to say goodbye for he was being sent to Australia. This was the last time I saw my Papa. The visit had been sweet but terribly short.

Papa was sent to Australia on a terrible ship called *The Dunera*, a name that will be remembered with shame. This ship was manned by British soldiers who treated men like my Papa abominably. They stole the few belongings these poor men had and took the food, so that the rations given out were much too small. They had not, however, dealt with someone like my Papa. He and two friends decided they would volunteer to be cooks, this way they had enough to eat, and of course when in charge of the kitchen, all the other men too ate much better. None of this did I learn from Papa, but read in the book, *The Dunera Internees*, when it was given me in 1981.

I had again to cope with learning English and keeping my mouth shut whenever mother blamed me for something I didn't do. I was no angel, but tried very hard to keep the peace. By now I had learned that if father took my side in an argument, she made him suffer with her waspish tongue which was the last thing I wanted.

Being a good Jewish family, we went to the synagogue on Saturday morning. Father and I to say our prayers, mother to show off her clothes and gossip. It was a beautiful building which I came to love. I felt at home hearing the prayers in Hebrew. It reminded me of Hoof where going to the synagogue had been so much part of my life. On Sunday morning in Swansea as at home, we went to Chader, Sunday School in English. When I first went to Hebrew classes, I was very disappointed. I had thought I would learn more than I already knew. This sounds very conceited but was merely how I felt. The teacher was very fond of hitting his pupils across the knuckles when they made a mistake. This did not happen to me. I could not speak English but my Hebrew was good and the teacher could not fault my reading. Slowly it dawned on me that the lessons had become very boring for I was not learning anything new. One Sunday I managed to find father alone and somehow made him understand that there was nothing more I could learn. The next Sunday morning he came with me to classes. Despite dirty looks from the teacher, he stayed and saw for himself. What was said between my father and the teacher I do not know, but each Sunday after that we would go for our walk to the beach.

At school, I learned to speak English quickly for the reason that by this time war had broken out and I did not want to be made to feel different. The few months since my arrival in Wales I had of course been different, but nobody had blamed me for that. They thought I was a bit of a freak, but harmless. Now anything German was anathema to all. I was very lucky. Mother, though born of Polish parents, had been born and educated in London. Dear father, born in Russia and speaking no English when he arrived in Britain as a very young man, made very sure that he taught himself English without any accent – quite an achievement. So it wasn't very long before I spoke English more like a native of England than of Wales.

Childhood in Wartime Swansea

TIME WENT BY and I heard nothing of Mutti and the children. They were always in my heart and thoughts. I worried about them. When war broke out I did not expect to hear from Germany. I found life very difficult in many ways. I couldn't manage to please mother, but I took that in my stride. Now I loved school, so no trouble there. Father, as long as mother was not around, showed me love and affection. We both knew that no emotion could be shown unless we were alone. We lived in the centre of Swansea, so when the bombing started we went into the cellar which father had had reinforced. The dreadful sounds of the bombers and the bombing were very frightening. Many hours were spent in the cellar. When the bombing was at its worst we crossed the road at a run into the air raid shelter opposite the house.

So life went on. School, sirens, bombs. That was the way the days passed. At the beginning of the war, if we were in school, each girl was allocated another girl who lived near the school and as soon as the sirens wailed we went with our partners to her house and stayed until the 'all clear' sounded. At home of course it was the cellar or the big shelters.

Hours, days and weeks past. I had reached my 11th birthday. Never before had I celebrated a birthday. There had been no time for such trivia. This was very different. On my birthday, my dear girls in the workshop gave me a present, a funny animal. It had a stuffed head and you put your pyjamas into his tummy. It was a panda. I was overwhelmed and hugged them all. My present from mother and father was a book of all things. I had only started learning English in June, now in January I was given a book for a gift. The book was Charles Dickens' 'David Copperfield'. Not only was it difficult English, it had tiny print, which was almost unreadable. My greatest joy was the gift given to me by Phyllis and Dave. They gave me my very first watch which I loved so much I was afraid of wearing it in case something bad should happen to it. Not that mother allowed me to wear it except as a great treat. Dave used to take Phyllis to the theatre each Saturday night when he would buy her a box of 'Black Magic' chocolates. The box of chocolates turned into two smaller boxes when, at their request, I was allowed to go with them each week. There was nothing in my life then to compare with those wonderful Saturday nights. We sat in the same seats each week: the 'Orchestra Stalls'. I could not understand what was said, but these treats started my lifelong love of music. The musicians made a pet of me. Every Saturday I left the theatre with more chocolates than I had going in. Of course I gave them to Phyllis, no way was I giving them to mother.

The following year passed quite quickly. Air raids, bombers overhead, all the terrors these involved. Home life went on as usual. No love, no affection just tension between mother and me, which never seemed to ease. I had learned English and mother thought it time for me to learn something which would be of use to them later in my life. So I was sent to a Commercial College. I was twelve years old. The new subjects were not only Shorthand and Typing, but included the normal High School curricula; History, which I loved, Geography, which I hated and many other subjects normally taught in Secondary School. The thing that hurt me most was mother looking over my shoulder saying 'You must work harder, we are paying for this education'. These continual comments were quite unnecessary for I was working as hard as I could. What they succeeded in doing was to make me very angry, so much so that out of sheer rage I worked harder than ever before, determined to pass every examination. I was never brilliant, just very angry.

Soon after my 13th birthday in January, I received a letter from the German Red Cross. It informed me that Mutti, Rolf, Heinz, Sally, Ruth, Ludwig and Zilla had been in the first group of deportees sent by cattle truck to Riga, in Latvia. As far as the Red Cross was concerned all my family had perished. The deportation happened in December 1941. I ran to my room followed by mother. (No one leaves a room without explaining the reason.) I gave her the letter, which of course she could not read. After translating it for her, I pushed her out of the door. I lay on my bed and cried and cried until I thought my heart would break. Some time after, as soon as I was able, I went downstairs. For the first time father took me in his arms and held me. I needed it very badly. Mother stood glaring at me, father for once did not care, my need was greater than her anger. Father was no coward; he just hated the scenes mother made if she was displeased. That letter haunted me. I read it a thousand times. I hated reading it, yet something forced me to read and reread this awful piece of paper.

A few weeks later, Hitler, for once, did me a favour. He bombed our house and destroyed my hateful piece of paper. The bombing was dreadful; the bomb that destroyed our house fell directly on to the reinforced part of the cellar. We were lucky and crawled out from under the debris safe and sound. We spent the rest of that night in one of the big shelters across the road. As always the shelter was jam packed with people. Some of whom had been there all night and perhaps, like us, had their houses destroyed. What I remember most was the way people reacted to their loss and fear. No one sat and cried, they made the best of what tragedy they had suffered. Many times I heard people say 'We were lucky none of us was killed. It was only a house and can be replaced'. Many comments like that remain in my memory. I felt their loss and could not really understand their cheerfulness. To me the loss of our house was a reminder of the home I had lost in Hoof. I never could think of the big house in Swansea as home. Home was with my children, either in the hovel in Hoof or the misery of the orphanage. These were not good memories but only with my children could any place be called home. Next morning we left the shelter. What faced us was what was left of the house. It looked like a pile of rubble. When it was declared safe, we returned and saved what we could. Father's workshop, which was at the back of the house, seemed intact and with help he managed to salvage the machines with which he made his living. Mother naturally went to save her jewellery and her clothes. I climbed over the bricks and rubble; my room had been hit and I was desperate to find just two things, the photograph of my family and my panda. After a lot of searching the photograph turned up. It was still in the little case I had brought with me. I had treasured it all this time. My poor panda had been torn to shreds. Eventually I sewed it together and kept it for the children I hoped to have one day.

We spent a few days with friends of the family. Mother had many acquaintances but few friends. Those she did have were all her age. This was one of the reasons I had few Jewish friends. However, there was one family I loved very much, the Wolfs and they had two children: Alfie, who was some years older than me, and Rhona who was a few years younger. Many nights during the blitz we slept three in one bed. Thankfully their house escaped the bombs. We stayed with them until two rooms were found out of town, in a lovely place called Langland. I loved it, but it was not very comfortable, especially for mother. She spent her time moaning as if it was father's fault. At least I was left in peace for the moment. Each morning I walked to Oystermouth which was quite a trek. From there, I would take the Mumbles train to town and again walked till I came to my college. Before we were bombed, I had only a few friends, mainly from school. The age gap of my parents made it difficult to mix with Jewish children of my own age. I met some in the synagogue but this beautiful building was bombed very early during the war, so instead we used a very large house as a synagogue. Here one did not chatter, at least we were not allowed to. This makes me sound like a goody, goody child. Since I was very small, as I have said, I had learned Hebrew and knew how to follow the services on Saturday and all the Holy Days. I loved all the services and went to the synagogue to pray. After all, I had so much to pray for. I prayed that the Red Cross was wrong and my family was alive. Even though I knew in my heart that this was not so, but I needed the hope to cling to. I prayed for Papa, that he would stay well and perhaps send for me to join him in Australia. Another pipe dream. And I prayed that mother would treat me as if she loved me. I thanked the Lord that father was the man he was. I had a lot to pray for and knew in my heart that most of these prayers were in vain. Although I could not put my thoughts into words, I knew I had great faith, faith in God which has never left me throughout my life.

Things were made more difficult because there was no-one with whom I could talk or who could understand my misery and loneliness. I knew of only two other refugees in Swansea. One was named Erika, a little older than me. She had come to Swansea before me and had the advantage of being able to speak English. She had come from Vienna and for some reason always looked down on me. Making friends with her was impossible. She had also started in Terrace Road School but had won her Scholarship and went on to a Grammar school. I believe she went on to University. The other refugee was a boy called Henry. He too had come to Swansea earlier than I and he too could speak some English when he came. I could not make friends with him, this time for a different reason. He too came to a childless elderly couple. They owned a jewellery shop, were great snobs and mixed with only the very wealthiest people in town. Mother and father did not come into this category. This situation made it impossible for him and me to become friends. Added to all these problems was the fact that to the best of my knowledge their background and mine were so very different. I did discover, no idea how, that both these youngsters had their passage paid for by their parents. My loneliness and isolation was complete. There was no-one to whom I could talk of my past or my miserable present.

When we moved I had a whole new group of friends. Each day was fun. The Mumbles train and the weather had a lot to do with it. The train ran besides the sea. If the weather was rough we would be shaken about all over one another. When calm we could chatter on about something and nothing the way young people do today. To me the greatest joy was not being alone, not being shouted at for what I had or had not done. School in itself was no hardship. I have never been academically brilliant but became very miserable and very obstinate. The trouble was mother. If she did not find me doing my homework the moment I came through the door, she would point her finger at me and say, 'We are paying for your education and not for you to play'. She said it time and time again until she even made me feel guilty about going with the gang to the cliffs and swimming. This lady had no heart, no idea that a child of fourteen needed to do more than just work. Yet, I worked very hard at school. It really was not easy learning shorthand, typing and a myriad of different subjects when this had to be done in a language that was still being learned. For instance, spelling. English is a very hard language to spell. Somehow, miraculously I always came first in the class in spelling, I spelled every word phonetically, as I would have done had I been learning in German. It took me a very long time to learn the many subjects that were set for me, to gain all the diplomas I was determined to have. But mother's 'We are paying for this,' put iron into my soul and eventually I did gain the diplomas, more even than were expected from me.

Whilst living in little Langland, so very near the sea, I came to love the water and the swimming. The cliffs we climbed were covered with lichens and plants not found anywhere else. Beautiful small flowers I had never seen before. The most delightful finds were in the rock pools I loved to poke about in to find sea anemones, small crabs, seaweed that had bladders which gave a very satisfying plop when squeezed. So many new discoveries. The sea, in all its moods, a joy always. I loved it best when it was wild and the spray would almost reach the topmost rocks. It was a new world for me. I am sure it also had to do with the boys and girls who were my companions. The boys teased me and the girls accepted me as one of them.

I had always had a passion for reading. It was my way of escaping from the misery of mother. I had found a little library in town which was just opposite Clark's College so it was easily accessible for me during break times to pop across the road. Here, for very little, one could borrow all sorts of books. With no one to advise me, I took pot-luck. Read Rider Haggard, the plays of Shakespeare, anything and everything was escapism when written in a book. When mother upset me too much, I would take a book and escape where she could not find me. Up in the tallest tree no one could see me or hear me. At last I had found somewhere I could enjoy my books in peace. Of course there was a price to pay. Nagging, nagging until father would put his foot down and say 'enough'.

Nothing lasts and soon we moved back to another part of town, to a suburb of Swansea called Sketty. We settled in a delightful little house, one in a terrace of four. Opposite were allotments. I made friends with the men whose pride and joy these little plots of earth were. They so enjoyed digging. I was very shy and would stand silently watching, never saying a word. I do not know what it was about me that made these men want to talk to me and give me gifts of whatever fruit and vegetables were in season. Perhaps it was my very shyness that attracted them. Rationing was in force and food was not that plentiful. They were very competitive. Each man's plot was his pride and joy and each vegetable had to be the best. They made me feel very ordinary and they just seemed to like me – not something I was used to, I did not meet many grown-ups I could talk to without embarrassment.

When we moved to Sketty, I joined the Jewish youth club where I made friends mainly with girls. The only Jewish boys I liked were older than me and not interested in a 14-year-old girl. I wasn't keen on the boys of my own age, even those who liked me. I remember one instance, which shows my feelings. One of the boys wanted to kiss me but I did not want to be kissed, I did not like him. He had his friend hold my arms and again tried. Poor lad, he did not know me. I hit him so hard, he lost one of his front teeth. Rarely did I have trouble again. I did like some of the non-Jewish boys I met, but this was a big taboo. No Jewish girl was allowed to go out with a non-Jewish boy. I remember whilst still living in Langland being taken to the very small local cinema by a non-Jewish boy I liked. We sat in the back row, kissing and cuddling and smoking a small cigarette, a Woodbine, all he could afford. I looked up to see one of mother's cronies watching me, then leaving the cinema as fast as she could run. When I arrived home, mother stood on the doorstep wagging her finger and shouting on top of her voice of the sin I had committed. She shouted till she was hoarse. I said nothing, just let it flow over my head. At least this time I knew I had deserved her displeasure which in itself was unusual. No, I would not answer her when she wanted a promise that this would never happen again. It was easier to say nothing.

Growing Up

WHILST BEING PART of the Jewish Youth Club, I was selected to represent the club at the Swansea Youth Council because I had learned shorthand and typing which was deemed useful for a secretary. The day I joined the Council was the luckiest day of my life. I met Jean who was eighteen months older than me. We had nothing in common except that she lived with a step-mother who was not unkind, but they did not have anything in common. I, of course, had mother. We became instant friends and have stayed friends to this day. She it was who, in difficult times, made my life worth living, asking nothing from me but friendship, which was given wholeheartedly. We stayed on the Council together and soon she became Chairman while I was re-elected as secretary. The only time anyone ever heard my voice was when I read out the minutes, other than that I never spoke, was much too shy. We enjoyed one another's company. Not even mother could part us had she wanted to. Many times I went to Jean's home; never did she come to mine. No friends of mine ever came to our house. My friends were not welcome, mother made this very clear. I eventually came to call Jean's mother 'ma' and we became very fond of one another. I think this was because there was nothing we wanted from each other. I was always made very welcome in her house.

Time flew. Soon I left Clarks College with all my diplomas. Father was delighted, though there was not one word of praise from mother. I was so very proud when I went for an interview for my first job. Having good qualifications, I was offered twenty seven and six pence. At last I would be away from mother for days, at last would have some money of my own. The Gods must have been laughing. Two weeks later father was taken ill and, too soon, he died. I was broken-hearted and mother shouted at me that it had nothing to do with me. The only peace I had had was in his company; the only affection had come from him when she was not around. How I loved that man, and now I had lost him and was alone with my nemesis.

At fifteen I took over the business. The girls working in the workshop were all old enough to be my mother. Unfortunately, the girls from the old house had left one by one. Some had gone into munitions factories where they could earn much more money. So now once again I had other helpers. We worked very well together, I think they were sorry for me and made my life as easy as they could. I needed all the help I could get. I ordered stock, kept books and looked after the customers, the bit I loved most. I have always enjoyed meeting people. After our house was bombed, father had found two rooms almost opposite to where we had lived. On the ground floor was a Monumental Mason named Nurse and Payne. We were upstairs in two rooms and a little kitchen. So small two people would have filled it to capacity. If we needed the toilet, we had to go outside summer and winter. This caused great inconvenience but was also fun. Two boys, brothers named Denzil and David Smith, worked downstairs, or rather, outside in a shed. Delightful boys, how they liked to tease us, me especially, I was still so very shy. Soon after I had to take charge of the business, I found that I could go through the back shed, directly into the back of Woolworths where there was a Tea and Coffee Bar. This changed my life in odd ways. Yet again I made new friends, one especially, a man, not a boy, a man named Peter who had been invalided out of the RAF. We became good friends. He teased me endlessly. He bought me my coffee each morning, took me to the cinema. I making sure never to be discovered: he making fun of this conspiracy in which he took great pleasure. We stayed friends for over twenty years. The most important gift that Peter gave me was to treat me like a grown up. The girls who worked in Woolworths became friends, especially the girls who worked on the cosmetic counter. Any time some lipstick or make up came into the store, one of the girls would call me and offer me an Outdoor Girl lipstick. It was the first and least expensive lipstick on the market. For me this was a terrific treat. I had never had a lipstick, mother would not have approved. Now I felt very grown up, even though I could only wear it out of her sight.

Mother had never worked and was not about to start. After work I would go home, to cook, clean, polish and wash. While mother would go around the house with a white cloth to see if there was any dust. There was never a time in our joint lives that we agreed on anything. Not even when she knew that what I had said was correct. Now it went from bad to worse. There was no father to take into consideration, she was in charge and I was the slave. If I dared to query anything she would say, 'You ungrateful child, if it had not been for me you would be in the Gas Chambers with your family'. Always, these words left me helpless. Was she right? If she was, then I wished she had never saved me and I had died with my Mutti and my children. If we argued then again and again she would say these hurtful words. She did not care how much they hurt me.

There was little joy in my life. But there was one thing I loved to do which did give me pleasure and that was to dance. I had learned ballroom dancing at Oystermouth Youth Club and had loved to dance ever since. Mother had a nephew, some eight years older than I. He too loved dancing. From time to time, he would ask me to go to dances with him. We mainly went to the Patti Pavilion. A beautiful dance floor where dancing was a joy. There was only one drawback, if another man asked me to dance, Sid would stand at the edge of the floor and glare until the dance was finished, then would take my arm and lead me away as if he owned me. This did not please me one bit and I told him so. He would sulk, not a pretty sight, and refuse to take me dancing again. I always pretended that it did not matter, but missed the dancing very much. Within days Sid was back, once again wanting to take me to the Patti. I always pretended reluctance, but was never very good at pretending. In fact, was really very naïve. I still went to the cinema with other boys, but was always careful not to be seen.

Friends of mother's had moved to Birmingham after they had been bombed here in Swansea. She and I went to visit. There I met a Jewish boy who I liked, more than liked, he was my first love. Some of his family still lived in Swansea, so he came to visit quite often. We became very close. At last I had found someone to love and be loved by in return. I was so fortunate, even his parents liked and approved of me. I became very fond of them. Unfortunately, he had two more years of university to do to qualify as an optician. I tried very hard to be patient. Our meetings were too few. When he did come to Swansea, we would meet in the park. I recall once being invited to dinner at his aunt's house, on a Friday night. Aunt and uncle were very orthodox; we had our meal. By now, it was dark. But in this house, no light was allowed to be put on. We sat for some hours in candle light, not able to make small talk for we had nothing in common with these two strange people. We had both been brought up in homes where religion was rather lax. Sitting in the dark with these strange people was very uncomfortable. We left as soon as it was polite to do so. We walked the dark streets and enjoyed just being together.

Meanwhile mother's viciousness became harder and harder to bear. She had learned of my budding romance and was determined not to lose her skivvy to any boy. I was only seventeen, but she was taking no chances. She kept me busy and watched me like a hawk. I had to account for any time I was not working, except when I went dancing with Sid which was fine by her. The dancing, she felt, was safe and involved no danger of her losing her slave. I even tried to join the Land Army. I knew I was not old enough to join any of the other forces and was desperate to get away. As always, I was too trusting. I had forgotten that mother always went through my pockets and drawers. I had received a letter from the Land Army asking for more details. Mother found this letter and all hell broke loose. She shouted, ranted, raved until I could stand it no longer and had to withdraw my application. She had even consulted our solicitor who had told her that she could insist that I was her only means of support. My fate had now been sealed and she kept me with her. She thought there was no way I could leave my life of servitude.

How wrong she was. I was in my eighteenth year. Life had not got any better, if anything it was worse. Nothing I did seemed to please. There is only so much a human being can take. I was at my wits' end, nowhere to turn, no one except my Jean to talk to. I truly believe that were it not for our friendship... well, there were times I contemplated suicide. How one human being can treat another with such disregard of their feelings I will never know?

Marriage

IN MY INNOCENCE, I had never realised that Sid loved me. It had never occurred to me for he had never spoken of his feelings. He was the son of mother's sister. Born when she was in her 40s. This lady was unlike her sister in appearance but so alike in nature. Vicious, demanding always needing to be the centre of attention. Her husband was her exact opposite. Kind and gentle and loving. He was a first class tailor and worked with his eldest son, Sam. A man as strange as the rest of the family. A complete loner. Neither he nor his wife visited anyone nor was anyone welcome in their house. This was where father-in-law spent his time, for here was the workshop where the very elegant suits were made. My father-in-law to be, spent all the day and half the night with Sam working very hard. He stayed late each day because he did not wish to go home and spend time being nagged or completely ignored. This dear man had come, as had father, from Russia. On arrival in London, he was asked his name. He told the man in charge that his name was Lisagurski. As the official could not spell it, he told this bewildered man that from now his name was Lewis, and Lewis it stayed. Sid had two sisters, Bessie and Sadie, both much older than himself. Bessie was the eldest. Both these sisters were superb pianists. Bessie taught music and in the evenings they would play in cinemas where silent films were shown. All this was before my time. Sid, his mother and father had been bombed out whilst living in the town. Subsequently, they moved into Bessie's large house in the Uplands area of Swansea. Bessie's husband, another delightful person, was not best pleased. He saw through his mother-in-law and disliked her heartily, but had to hide his feelings, a difficult thing to do for he was a very outgoing person, a salesman for a paint company. There was also a daughter, Jacky, extremely spoiled, five years younger than me. Now their house was very full. Sam, Bessie and Jacky had the main part, whilst mother and father had the middle room and a bedroom, plus of course a bedroom for Sid, the spoiled son. They seemed to rub along.

This then was Sid's family, a very mixed bunch. As his sisters were so much older, they treated him as a child which meant he had three mothers and was completely and utterly spoiled. The only scholastic qualification he possessed fitted him for nothing more than a secretary. He worked for a removal company. Yet despite living at home and having no expenses, he made very little money. None of this occurred to me at the time. I was too young and too naive. During the war, Sam and Sid somehow avoided being called up for the services.

One day Sid and I went to the park and sitting on a bench he said out of the blue 'Mother thinks it a good idea if we got married'. This remark should have taught me something. There was no word of love or affection. I thought his mother hated me. So what was all this about. He was my dancing partner, I had never considered him as a partner for life. I went home and did a lot of thinking. I did say I was naïve. My thought ran along the lines of: he is so much older than me, so he will look after me and I can rely on him. How wrong can one be; I was kidding myself. I did not want him as a husband; I desperately wanted to get away from mother, desperately wanted children to replace the children I had lost. I was fond of him. What did I know of love and marriage? Yes, I still had thoughts of my first and only love. At 18 what can one know of love? After a long deliberation, I said I would marry him. He presented me with a beautiful engagement ring which made me feel very proud, very grown up. I am sure part of this pride was the feeling that at last I could get away from mother who of course hated the idea. She was losing her skivvy and would have no one to do her bidding, no one she could bully. By this time, thoughts of leaving her were thoughts of heaven.

At the time, 1948, the age of consent was twenty-one. Therefore it was important for me to have my Papa's consent to this marriage. Papa and I had corresponded during these years, many of which he had spent in an atrocious camp for aliens in the desert of Australia. Eventually when this camp was closed, he had moved to Melbourne, where he went to work for a man who manufactured paper. The type used for wrapping and paper bags. Our letters were few and really said nothing. He did not tell me of the atrocious conditions in which he had to live. I, not to worry him as I thought, told him nothing of the misery of my existence. Once he started working, he began to send me tins of fruit, much more welcome were the infrequent letters. Now I wrote to him asking permission to marry Sid. He replied giving me his permission, enclosing a small cheque and telling me he had just remarried himself. That was the last letter I ever received from him. During the years to come, I wrote repeatedly. First sending photographs of my wedding, subsequently photographs of my children. I sent letters by special delivery, registered mail and eventually by hand. I know these were delivered. But no reply ever .

To do mother justice, she arranged a grand wedding on the 27 May 1948. War had ended in 1945, but everything was on coupons and food still rationed. She managed to find a way around this somehow. My bottom drawer consisted of two of everything, the very minimum she could get away with. The wedding itself was a great event to show people how generous she was. It turned out a complete fiasco. Our marriage took place in the Masonic Hall where Sam was a member. Food was laid out as a buffet, all home made. She was a wonderful cook and, by now, I could match her cooking, I had had enough practice. We had cooked and baked for weeks. I looked forward to it but she hated every minute she spent working for the time she would lose her skivvy. She had found a dressmaker to make my wedding dress. This lady apparently had a wonderful reputation. It was a shame she had to spoil it with my dreadful dress. Anything that could go wrong with this dress, went wrong. I hated it on sight. Each fitting something else was not right. Mother was the cause of most of this hassle. Nothing could please her. I had no say in anything, I had to stand there like a tailor's dummy being told to stand still, turn around. Then came the problem of the veil. Not even mother could find lace for a veil. Until eventually from somewhere she found some parachute silk. However, the dress-maker wouldn't have anything to do with this. I had always been a good needlewoman, so it fell to me to make it. I embroidered it with great loving care and it became, to me, a thing of beauty, admired by all who saw it. At last I had something of my own with which not even mother could find fault.

When at last the great day arrived, I felt like an animal prepared for slaughter. I was made to sit absolutely still like a doll. Nothing must mar this day for mother. She had come to terms with the fact that not even she could stop this event from happening, so it had to be perfect. I had two bridesmaids. One was a dear friend named Myra, the other was Jacky. She and I had never become friends. Mother chose her for me; what choice did I have? They both looked beautiful and I, hating to look in a mirror, felt frumpish. I hated my dress, was tired of mother's fussing and bullying, perhaps apprehensive too. What did I know of marriage and, in particular, sex. My sex education consisted of mother telling me that I must take a piece of a sheet with me in case I bled. I had no idea why I should bleed, no idea what to expect from marriage. Perhaps apprehensive's too mild a word. I was terrified of the unknown. In my time, sex was not a subject to be discussed. As I sat there like a miserable doll, a memory came to mind. Years earlier when my periods started, mother was in the shop, and I had to go to the toilet outside. Suddenly I started to bleed. I ran inside and told mother I was bleeding to death. All she told me was how to use an old towel when this happened once a month and if a boy kissed me I would become pregnant. How was that for sex education? Eventually when she left the shop, one of the girls came in from the workshop. They had heard what mother had said to me and wanted to explain that what she had said was wrong. Perhaps if the girls had been with me on this occasion, I would not have been so afraid of the unknown.

By the time the car came for us I was a nervous wreck. Mother had not stopped fussing for one minute and I wished her anywhere except with me. We arrived at the Masonic Hall which was filled with so many people they scared me. Some I knew, many I did not. Mother had invited all the Jewish community: to show off and for the gifts she was sure we would receive. I would have given anything to flee. First, we had to have the civil ceremony. Next we had to go under the Chupa – a silk cloth held up with four poles which represents a tent. As I did not have two parents, Sam and Bessie stood in for the next part of the ceremony. They walked me around the Chupa a number of times, then I went to Sid's side and the ceremony started. In Hebrew of course. After Sid had broken the glass, it was wrapped in a cloth for good luck. The ceremony was over, but the worst was yet to come. All these milling people, wishing us good health, which I am sure they meant; more and more people coming up to us. The hall was spinning about me. I hadn't realised, nor had mother cared, that I had not eaten all day and it was now about seven in the evening. It was a wonder I hadn't fainted. The evening passed, people, music, dancing. I who loved dancing, hated every moment of it. It went on for hours. We were not allowed to leave until the last guest had gone. Sometime during the evening I heard a commotion in the corner where the bar had been set up. My brothers-in-law, Sam and Sadie's husband Lou, were in charge. I learned much later that at a certain time, mother had decided enough wine and spirits had been consumed and the bar was to close. People went to the bar for a drink and to their horror Sam and Lou had to refuse to serve them. Mother wanted to return as much as possible from where it came. Saving money of course. This caused such animosity between the two men and mother that they didn't talk to her for some years.

Midnight came and all the guests had gone. I was pleased and thankful for the silence. Sam took Sid and me in his car to the Mermaid Hotel, Mumbles, where we were shown to our room. I who was afraid of very little, became apprehensive. What now? I found out soon enough. No love, no tenderness, no affection. Now, horrified, I learned that my new husband was not capable of these emotions. Sid had never been with a woman before and I was the complete innocent. He seemed to give no thought to my feelings at all. Once he was satisfied, he turned over and went to sleep. It was the most dreadful night of my life. I lay very still in the bed, listening to a man snoring like a loud machine. Eventually I got up and sat in the window of the room for the rest of that night. Watching the beautiful sun rise over the bay, I said to myself 'You have made the biggest mistake of your life'.

Next day we went to Bournemouth for our honeymoon. Nothing changed my opinion of the first night. Some months before our wedding, Sid had bought a book on 'love and marriage'. We both read it. What knowledge he managed to garner from it, I have no idea. I know it made no sense to me. The first night and the rest of the honeymoon proved to me that Sid, although he had read the book, had learned no more from it than I had. The hotel in which we stayed was of course Jewish. One could not find Kosher food in any other hotel. The other visitors were all elderly people. A pianist played classical music every afternoon. Although we both loved music, my taste was for classics, dance music and jazz. Sid, although we danced to the music, only enjoyed the classics. As much as I would have liked to stay and hear the music, I had to find a quiet spot and a soft chair. I needed to be alone and was desperately sore. My faulty kidneys were causing me great pain. I had tried explaining this to my husband, but he just ignored me. I tried to find some books. Maybe Jewish people did not read on their holidays? There were no books to be found. The youngest person in the hotel was the manager. I approached him begging for something to read. Eventually, he gave me some of his own books. A motley selection, but I would have read anything, even a shopping list. There was something in me that needed a book of any description as long as it allowed me to block out what was happening. After listening to the music for some time, Sid would come looking for me. We would go up to our room and the agony would start all over again. Some afternoons we walked amongst the pine trees – never long enough for me. We saw nothing of the town. It was a very, very long week. I wasn't happy until we were on our way back to Swansea. I now realise, looking back as I write this, that each train journey seems to have been spent in silence. On the journey to Bournemouth, I think we were both too tired and I too distressed. The return journey was no better. We had nothing in common. Dancing and music are not enough subjects from which one can make small-talk.

When we arrived back home, Sam was waiting for us to take us to Sadie and Lou's house where we were to stay whilst looking for a place of our own. Sid had given up his own job. Sadie, who had a business in a town called Llanelli, had given it to my husband as a wedding present. For a while the pair of them went each day to Llanelli, 12 miles from Swansea and I was left to find a house. I tried very hard. At the time, after the war, it was difficult to find houses for sale. When Sadie and Sid returned each day, I had house hunted, cooked and cleaned. Nothing very much had changed.

Eventually I found a house that Sid and the rest of the family approved of mainly because it was not too far from where they lived. At last, I was pleased to have somewhere of my own. A little privacy was a rare gift for which I longed. We had to furnish the house but all goods were on coupons and this did not make life easy. Sid had very few friends, but one of them owned a furniture shop. At last some luck and with the minimum of furniture, we moved into our own home. During this time, I had gone with Sid to run the shop which was not as simple as it sounds. We lived in the west part of Swansea, the railway station was a long way on the east side which meant taking a bus, then a forty minute train journey to Llanelli and from that station, again, a long walk to the shop. There I worked all day in a workshop with four girls. Very quickly I realised that my husband knew nothing about the business and was actually finding it impossible to get on with the girls. Even customers seemed to scare him. Once again I was a skivvy. This time it was even worse, I had to be a dutiful wife as well, and a housekeeper. Again I was in servitude. I had no preconceptions about marriage, but I had not anticipated the pain involved.

In the family I had now joined, Sid's mother was the boss.

Nothing was done without her approval or consent. She treated me mostly as if I did not exist, which was fine by me. We had hated one another on sight and I was quite pleased when I did not have to speak to her. I think that my husband had told her of my being a reluctant wife. She kept making snide remarks, not to me, but at me. She could no more understand my reluctance which was allied to pain, than Sid had.

I now had a house I wanted to turn into a home. It was large with a beautiful view. There were no modern appliances. My kitchen had a stone floor, a very deep old fashioned sink, a cooker, a walk-in pantry, a table and one kitchen cabinet. That was my lot. All the other rooms had lino floors which had to be highly polished, as did most everything else. I was looking forward to spending time making a home of my own. It was July, when I suddenly noticed my periods had stopped. I knew a great deal about babies, but nothing of conception. By August I was really worried. I did not want to go to our own surgery where all the doctors were male. I was very shy and the idea of a male doctor examining me was not something I could tolerate. I went to a woman doctor who had been recommended to me but whom I did not know. I went with great trepidation. Of course I wanted children, but this was too soon. My husband and I had never discussed the matter. To my delight the doctor informed me that I had a 'growth'. I went away quite happily and told my husband what I had done. I was right; he didn't want children. Not that he took precautions. I had had to have a coil fitted when we returned from 'the honeymoon'. It was very uncomfortable and painful but I had had no choice, Sid had insisted. I think by this time, with mother and now a demanding husband, I had become so used to obeying orders. Two months passed and I was putting on weight. Of course, now I knew I must be pregnant, but could not tell my husband. He would have had to be blind not to know. As usual, what he did not want to know, he ignored. For me, being pregnant was a joy. I loved every moment of it. I was never sick. Everyone, except the family, told me how well I looked and that I glowed. I felt fit, well and very large. I was still making the trip to Llanelli and going to work. Soon however this had to stop. Sid had to cope on his own. What recriminations I had to put up with but I didn't mind. I was happily pregnant, had the house to myself all day and prepared a nursery. Painting the walls, climbing on ladders painting the ceiling, I had no idea that I could have caused any hurt to my baby. I was happy all day and the nights were peaceful except for the constant moaning of my husband.

Unfortunately, this was the time mother became very ill. She had pneumonia and pleurisy. There was no one to look after her. Her nieces did not like her and the friends she had could not have cared less. Once again it fell to me. Strangely, during the time since my marriage, I had not noticed how her attitude to me had changed. I did not see her very often and tried to avoid her company as much as I could. Each day I went to her house, looked after her, cooked, cleaned and did all that was necessary. Then I noticed how she reacted to me. No more 'Do this or that' now it was 'please and thank you'. All this took a while to sink in. I was no longer her slave; she was grateful for every small thing I did for her. Her thanks were sincere. Even the way she looked at me was different. No more hostility but actual affection. I put all this down to her illness and was surprised when she recovered and the affection was still there. In all honesty I cannot say that my attitude towards her had changed. Now, however, we seemed to be at ease with one another. To show her appreciation, she gave me my first piece of jewellery which I have never worn. Perhaps it was too difficult for me to believe that this particular leopard had changed her spots. As soon as she was better, I was once again on the old treadmill of my marriage.

During the months of my marriage, I had to do my shopping miles from where we lived. Food was still rationed and mother-in-law insisted that I shopped in a small corner shop near the town. If you were a regular customer, some little extra was forthcoming now and then. The shopkeeper had known the family for many years. As I had become, if reluctantly, part of the family, I too received a little extra. Since my pregnancy had become self evident, my bits and pieces were many and received with thanks. On the morning of the 21st March 1949, I awoke full of energy and decided to do my shopping. I took a bus to the nearest point to the little shop and walked the rest of the way. After a great deal of shopping, I ended up carrying two very heavy bags up the very steep hill to my house. When I had finished putting away the shopping, I decided to do my usual baking. Baked a whole tin of biscuits, my speciality, then decided I could see dust under the bed. With great difficulty I crawled under the bed to polish the lino. So far so good. When I had finished and tried to retreat the way I had come, I was in trouble. I was stuck. As hard as I struggled, I could not move. My stomach far gone with the baby was so big it was a miracle that I had managed to get under the bed in the first place. I struggled, and stopped to get my breath. By this time I had niggling pains, nothing much, just uncomfortable. Eventually, breathless and in some pain, I somehow managed to emerge from under the bed feeling triumphant. My back was hurting, I thought from my exertions. I had never truly known the date of conception, nor the date when the baby was due. After my performance under the bed, I went downstairs to prepare Sid's meal. He noticed nothing when he came home. Not my pain nor the fact that I seemed unable to catch my breath. All he cared about was eating the food in front of him. At about nine, I could not bear the pain any longer and asked Sid to go across the road and ring from our neighbours. Sam and Sid took me to the home where the Matron seeing that I had no energy even to speak sent them both away. My contractions were very frequent and painful by this time and I was taken to the delivery room. Ten minutes after twelve on the 22nd of March my daughter was born. I had had my 20th birthday on the 9th January, now I had my first longed for baby. After the birth, I was very woozy and two stout nurses wanted to carry me downstairs from the delivery room. I did not want to be carried, I wanted to walk. I am sure I had no idea that I was making such a fuss, but exhausted, I was eventually carried downstairs into a room with three other women. The next morning when I saw my baby for the first time I was horrified. No way could this wrinkled, ugly thing be mine. They had made a mistake and given me the wrong one. I had seen all the babies Mutti had given birth to and none looked like this wrinkled monkey. I really was very upset and wouldn't accept it. Matron explained that the baby was only four and a half pounds. This was why she was so wrinkled. She assured me that as soon as the baby put on weight she would look completely different. Reluctantly I put her to my breast. As she began to suck, the strangest thing happened to me. Never had I known such pleasure and satisfaction. It was sensual, I had never known what that meant. When she had finished her feed, I was very reluctant to let her go and wanted the wonderful feeling to go on for ever. No longer was she wrinkled and ugly, she was mine, all mine.

Mother wanted to know what we were going to call this baby. We had never discussed names. I therefore made my own decision and would not be moved from it. Firstly, I wanted to call her after my Mutti, whose name had been Hannah. But this was too old fashioned for the time. I also wanted a name to remind me of father whose name had been Hyman. I decided to call her Anita. The nearest I could get to both names. Reluctantly, both mother and mother-in-law agreed. After all I was not favouring anyone and the name was neutral.

When my husband eventually came to see me there was no word of congratulation, no word of affection. All he said was 'Thank heavens that is over'. When he was shown his daughter, no emotion crossed his face; this could have been anyone's child, he didn't seem to care. He did ask when I would be coming home. In those days after having a child, it was a two weeks' recovery period which did not please him one bit. Too bad. I can remember to this day what joy my baby gave me. No marriage could compare, in fact nothing I had ever known could compare to the love I felt for this small scrap of humanity that was my child.

By the time it was time for us to go home, she had put on two pounds and signs of her beauty were becoming very clear.

Mother-in-law had bought the baby the Rolls Royce of prams called the Sliver Cross. It was so large, it wouldn't go into a car and I had to walk home. Anita became my world. I did all the housekeeping, shopped with difficulty. The pram was very beautiful, but very heavy. Pushing it up the hill with a baby and all my shopping was, even for a youngster like me, formidable. I cooked my husband's meals, did all that was required to keep my house spotless. All done quite automatically. Nothing had any meaning except my very beautiful baby. People would stop me in the streets to admire her. I was so proud. She slept all day and screamed all night which drove Sid crazy. Not once did he pick her up, day or night.

I became very tired from the sleepless nights and Sid decided that the baby had had enough of my attention. It was time I returned to wifely duties. What a time to choose. Anita was only four weeks old when my husband decided it was time I resumed those wifely duties. My nights of peace were over. I still got up a dozen times a night to stop her crying but this was no hardship as I could hold her in my arms and derive comfort from her small body. As my daughter grew, mother-in-law started to tell me what I must do to make sure that her granddaughter was brought up correctly. This was the straw that broke my back. I had brought up five children almost from birth. Now this horrible woman was trying to imply that I did not know how to look after my own child. Goodbye mother-in-law, I had more than I could take from my husband. I would not tolerate her interference. I stayed away from their house for as long as I could. I was fonder of my father-in-law. I badly wanted to see him for I had come to love him dearly. Soon after my marriage, each time I had gone to their house I had automatically kissed dad on entering and when leaving. Only when I came to visit would he put down his Yiddish newspaper into which he escaped when he was at home. He adored Anita as he adored me.

When I had to stop working in the shop, (it was no place for an active baby), Sid bought me a machine that repaired nylon stockings. Nylons were very scarce, so ladies were only too pleased their stockings could be repaired. As Anita was such an active child I rarely had time to sit down never mind try to repair nylons which was a job that demanded great concentration. It was impossible for me to do this work during the day, so after I had taken Anita to bed, given Sid his meal, cleared up and washed the dishes, half the evening had vanished. I therefore spent half the night repairing stockings. Truly hard work. I had never been afraid of hard work but this work gave me miserable migraines. Concentrating so hard was also affecting my eyes. My night work had become a necessity. Sid had not managed to come to terms with running a business and cash was short.

What had happened to the life I had envisaged when I first accepted Sid's proposal? Where was the security and being looked after. My fears of that first night had come only too true. Soon nylons became plentiful, and repairing them not economically viable. Once again my husband found me something else to do. A Dutch firm had patented a machine that would repair materials such as tweed and the like, invisibly. I had to learn to work this machine. Nylon repairs had been hard, but this repairing was much harder. I had to learn to use this machine from the owners which took time and Sid, not the most patient person, would nag. How I hated the bitching and nagging. I'd had more than my share from mother. Here I was once again the victim. Why was I always a victim? I know I hated to fight, hated even more the sulks and demands that would ensue.

In 1951, I became pregnant again. Unfortunately, this was not to be my second child. At three months I had a miscarriage. My kidneys were giving me a great deal of trouble. The reason I was told for the miscarriage. To say that I was upset would be an understatement. Having children was what my life was for, I had tolerated a great deal of pain doing my wifely duties. I thought at least I would be rewarded with another child.

How I had missed in my life having someone to whom I could turn. Now my need was even greater. Even Jean was not here for me to tell my troubles to. She was in Birmingham working as a teacher. My sigh of relief could have been heard miles away, when at last she returned. She was the one person who made all the difference in my life. My friend was a strange contradiction. She was very staid and very 'Welsh Baptist'. Yet I could tell her almost anything; whether she understood some of my troubles was not important, she was there and would listen and comfort me. I cannot imagine how I would have managed without her.

In all my life I have met just two Jewish men who were work shy. The first was my Papa, the second I had married. Now, besides wife, housekeeper, mother, I was also the breadwinner. By this time, I was so used to being used as a skivvy, what was new? I did what had to be done, not without disappointment. I had so wanted, needed, to be looked after, but it was not to be. I desperately wanted more children. But that seemed unlikely. I had been lucky to have my daughter Anita. My kidneys had been damaged by the truncheon beating. And I had paid a hard price for my pregnancy.

Then a miracle happened. A new Rabbi came to our Synagogue. He too had come from Germany via the Kindertransport. He was some seven years older than I. Married with two children, this man had come in time to save my sanity. He was someone who understood what I had gone through. He too was lost and lonely and needed someone to talk to who knew what loneliness was. We would meet in the park and talk, talk and keep talking. There was so much we both had bottled within. It was like finding another half of myself that had been missing for many years. Together we found understanding and company. It became a need to be together. We had made unhappy marriages, we both knew that we had to make the best of our lives. He stayed in Swansea for three years, the happiest years of my miserable life. We shared all our thoughts and feelings. No word of love was ever uttered by either of us. I did love him very much, but was afraid to say the words. Sid had made me feel unworthy of love, and unfortunately I believed this. My love did not say the words either. It took thirty-five years before I discovered why. He moved away to Southport to a better paid job. We missed one another badly.

Mother had decided she did not want to live alone any more and wanted to move to Southport herself where she had a brother. I have not mentioned this wonderful man, for I saw him very rarely. He was in the same business as father had been. Unfortunately, at the beginning of the war, his wife took their two daughters to America where, after sometime, she managed to get an American divorce and married again leaving uncle completely alone. I believe he saw his daughters just once again. How this man could have come from the same family as mother and mother-in-law is a miracle I have never managed to fathom. Mother decided that she and uncle would set up house together in Southport. What a disaster. As always she had to be boss and Uncle Morris had to do as he was told. He had lived alone for a long time and found this hard to bear. This loving man could no more tolerate her bullying than I had done.

During this time, Sid, Anita and I went to Southport for two holidays. It was sheer hell. I'd had enough of being abused verbally by my husband, to see uncle going through the same agony was unbearable. To be truthful, I had not visited the town to be with mother; I knew her company would not make a holiday enjoyable. I had come to be once more with the man I loved. My love and I managed to see one another twice more. We sat on a bench in the park and talked and talked. Too soon, our time was up and we had to return to our spouses. This must have been about 1953, the last time we saw one another. We went for one more holiday to Southport. Mother took great pleasure in telling me that the man I loved had emigrated with his family to America. There had been no goodbye, there was no word for the next thirty-five years. He was gone but never forgotten.

Nothing could stop me trying for another child. I became pregnant again in 1954. It was a very difficult time. Early in the year, Jean had met a boy and asked me if she could bring him to meet me. They came one evening. As soon as I opened the door, Ron and I started to laugh and could not stop. I think Jean thought us mad. We explained that we had known one another when we were about younger. Girls from Clark`s College used to meet a crowd of boys on the corner of Craddock Street by Ways the bookshop. I was very infatuated with a friend of his, so saw them quite often. Jean of course did not know of this nor did I know Ron`s surname. When she'd spoken of him to me, the name meant nothing. Some months later they became engaged and the wedding date was set. We had a dressmaker make her dress, I made every piece of her trousseau. I offered to hold the reception in my house. I cooked and baked for days and days. All went very well and everyone seemed to enjoy the occasion. I was like a proud parent and loved every minute of the day. I was very tired for I was already pregnant, but full of joy for Jean and Ron, and for myself at my pregnancy.

Which unfortunately did not go well. My kidneys were badly damaged and I spent a great deal of time in hospital. At one stage the doctors wanted to take one of my kidneys and my child away. I fought them every inch of the way. Poor Anita, each time the ambulance came to take me to hospital, she would cry pitifully. Each time Anita, nearly six, would say to me 'Mummy if this baby does not come now, tell them we do not want it'. Each time she was disappointed; she wanted this baby and hated my pain. After much time spent in hospital, at last I had Martin, my son. Immediately I forgot all my pains. I had my longed-for son. Having had four brothers I had so wanted to replace, a son was the closest I could come. Before Martin was born, I had made Sid promise that with money I had saved, penny by penny, he would send for a Mohl from London. When a Jewish boy is born he has to be circumcised by a special Rabbi. The nearest Mohl was in Cardiff. An old man who had caused many a baby boy a great deal of pain and mutilation. This I could not bear but like a fool I trusted my husband to carry out my wishes. Women are not allowed to attend this ceremony. As luck would have it, Martin was born rather small and a certain weight has to be reached by the baby before the circumcision can be carried out. Because of this my baby and I were still in hospital. The day came for the circumcision. I happened to leave the ward as the Mohl from Cardiff came up the stairs to perform the ceremony. I, who rarely lost my temper, now was ready to tear Sid from limb from limb. He had broken his promise to me for the last time. I'd never trust him again. Thank heaven the operation went well, otherwise I would not have been responsible for my actions. Of all the broken promises, for me this one was the most important.

I recovered from my confinement and once again I worked to feed and clothe my children and husband. I did not mind – perhaps that is a simplification – of course I minded, but could do nothing about it. As always with me, what could not be cured had to be endured. I had my lovely children, but I decided I wanted at least one more child. Against doctor's orders, I became pregnant again. Like Mutti, getting pregnant was no hardship. Unfortunately, at five months, I had a miscarriage. This time the specialist insisted that I be sterilised. In those days, one needed two doctors plus a specialist before this procedure could be performed. It was one of the most traumatic events of my life. I was only 29 and knew that I had no more chances to enlarge my family. I felt I was no longer a woman. To me it was the biggest disappointment of my life – excepting of course, my marriage.

When Martin was a year old, we found a wonderful nanny who would babysit for us. Sometimes we would visit the synagogue for social occasions. However, there was no enjoyment for me in going to a dance. If I were asked to dance by another man, Sid would stand on the edge of the dance floor and glare. Eventually, no man would bother to ask me. What joy was there for anyone seeing my husband looking his most disapproving at all and sundry. I felt as if I were a piece of furniture, owned and allowed only to be used by Sid. I had not learned how to be independent and stand up for myself. I so hated the constant rows and sulks, which were his way of making me feel guilty. I never knew why I should feel guilty and couldn't think of anything I had done wrong. What was the crime when another man asked me to dance; we danced, nothing more. Eventually, I gave up even wanting a small pleasure such as going to a dance, it was not worth the effort involved. Sid had never been popular in the congregation, in fact, like his mother and brother he was actively disliked. It did not help his image when people saw how he treated me in public. He rarely went to the synagogue. I, on the other hand, took my children, even when very young, to services and Anita to Sunday school classes. Father-in-law loved seeing me and his grandchildren in synagogue. He went to every service. He was truly a very religious and good man. What a shame he had to live most of his life at home without love. We loved him dearly and were never reluctant to show him our affection. I thought I was the only one unhappy in their marriage, what a shame I never considered what dad was feeling. Although I cannot think of anything more I could have done besides loving him.

At this time, I decided I had had enough of working at home for pennies. I had saved the enormous sum of £50 and had found something I thought would make money. I took my £50, opened a very small shop in St. Helens Road, opposite the old hospital. In magazines I had noticed that people were buying knitting machines – a new, economical way of knitting garments at home. I contacted the manufacturers and managed to purchase a few machines on credit. First I had to learn to use them. I had to go to London to do this. What a joy. The only time I had been to London was when I had arrived by train from Southampton. Then of course I had seen nothing, except the inside of the enormous hall and Paddington station. Now, for the first time I saw London. It was a revelation. I was met at the station by a representative of the knitting machine company. I had been truthful with them and told them I had never been to London before, and was sure I would get lost. They treated me royally. For the first time, I felt I was a very important person, a new experience for me. Learning to use these machines was not too difficult, not after learning invisible mending, which had ruined my eyesight. I spent a day in London, was even taken out to lunch. I returned by a late train to Swansea and tried hard to explain to Sid my wonderful experiences.

Unfortunately, I made a very big mistake when starting the business. Not knowing any better, I had put the company into joint names, thereby giving Sid access to the accounts. He was still working in Llanelli but things were not going well. As my business grew, he became jealous of my success. Subsequently, he decided to let his shop run down even more, until it had to be closed and he joined me in my business – sorry, our business. In my ignorance, I allowed him to keep the books and look after the banking.

Most of my adult life, I had one very steady ambition, one that I had never thought would come to fruition. I desperately wanted to see my grandparents once again. I had seen them last when I was seven years old. I knew I had lost Mutti and the children. Papa was lost to me. At last, for the first time I was making some money. I put aside a certain sum each month. Praying that at some future date I would have enough to fulfil my ambition and go to the Argentine. I had to work very hard. For, not only had I to sell the machines, I had also to teach my customers to use them. This took up any spare time, time I would have much preferred to spend with my children. Sid, as usual worked as little as possible. Soon after I started the shop, I realised I had no way of delivering the machines which were both heavy and clumsy. I made enquiries and decided to purchase a car. I had never been in debt in all my life. Now I was forced to purchase a car on hire purchase. Unfortunately I had never driven a car, therefore I had to learn and fast. The garage supplying the car was two doors away from my little shop. I was lucky, I knew the owner, a very amiable man. I had to wait three months for the car. The joke at the time was that you could purchase any colour car, but it had to be black, the only colour available. I managed to persuade the owner of the garage to loan me a car and one of his mechanics to teach me to drive. By the time my car arrived I had passed my driving test. Now I was busier than ever, selling, delivering and teaching customers to use the machines. Yes, I was successful, but at what cost.

Two years after I started the business, when I decided to check my bank account, I received the shock of my life. There was no money to go to the Argentine, only enough to take me from month to month and pay off my car. Sid had emptied the account which, of course, was in joint names. When I faced him with his deceit, despite evidence from the bank, he denied having emptied it. He continued to deny his thieving until I had to give up asking questions. I never did come to terms with this abominable act, and never was able to make my journey to see my grandparents.

Despite all this, the business flourished. I had two girls helping me and had to move to larger premises. Having help gave me more time to spend with my children. I made it a rule only to deliver two evenings a week. I had managed to teach Sid to use the machines, to enable him to do some of the deliveries and teaching. It was good to have the house to myself and be with the children. This state of affairs continued for another few years. Because I could not trust Sid, I now had to do the book-keeping myself. I was lucky I could do it at home, so I worked late into the night after the children were in bed. Unfortunately, my arthritis started about this time and the pain was unbearable. I carried on to the best of my ability. It was some years later when I had to go into hospital frequently for traction that I had to sell not the business, but merely the stock. Each time I had to go into hospital, usually for three weeks at a time, Sid made enemies out of my friends and customers.

The arthritis led to the end of my solo business career. I was forced to find a job working for someone else. I was lucky. I had become extremely efficient, so had little trouble finding another job. I have had many in my life, most of them enjoyable. The truth is I am not very good at idleness.

Discovering Relatives

WHILST CORRESPONDING WITH OMA AND OPA in Argentina, I had been told of an aunt and uncle who lived in Copenhagen, Denmark. I had no idea how this could be an aunt. Mutti only had one sister and she lived in Germany. I could only conclude that the relationship came from one of Oma's brothers or perhaps sisters. I knew nothing of family further back than my own grandparents. The Argentinian correspondent had given me the address. I wrote to them a few times and they replied asking me to come and visit them. No chance, no money.

I had been in correspondence with a German Lawyer called Herr Doctor Loeb who lived in London and represented many of the refugees in Germany who were able to claim reparation. A delightful little man – he really was very small, as was his wife. They lived in Golders Green, London. So when I had the chance eventually to visit London, I met them both for the first time. After many years of my lawyer writing and visiting Germany, things at last came to a surprising conclusion. I had many forms to complete, information to pass on until I thought there could not possibly be anything the German authorities did not know about me. Now they wanted to know where I had received my education. The name of the college and even the name of the headmaster. Mr Davies, the Head, had always taken a great interest in my education and was very proud when I passed all my exams. Now he sent me a copy of two letters. One he had received from Germany asking his opinion of my ability to go on to further education. The other was his reply. I was amazed and very pleased at this reply. He emphatically informed Germany that, had I had the opportunities denied me by circumstances, he was sure that I had had the ability to go on to university and attain whatever I set my mind on. I wrote and thanked him also expressed my surprise at his flattering comments. He replied to my letter informing me that he had done no more than write the truth. This very flattering comment had a very important effect on me. Suddenly, the derogatory remarks my husband so often made about my abilities, no longer had the same effect on me. If Mr Davies had so much faith in my abilities, who was Sid to keep putting me down. Now I stood up for myself, I think for the first time.

A letter arrived for me from Herr Loeb, my attorney, telling me that Germany had granted me the immense sum of £250 for 'loss of education'. I had never had so much money in my life and was certainly not putting it into the business as my husband wished. No way was this man getting his hands on my money yet again. I gave this immense amount of money a great deal of thought. I knew that for once I had to spend it on myself, otherwise Sid would soon get his hands on it and I would have nothing. Suddenly I thought of going to Copenhagen. I who had never been anywhere, decided I wanted to meet the only family I had closer than Argentina. My husband's disapproval and nastiness did nothing to change my mind. I wrote to Aunt Irma and Uncle Olaf asking if I might pay them a visit. The reply came back immediately. `When, how etc.` I booked a flight to Copenhagen. It had never occurred to me to fly, this really was something strange and outrageous, but I was determined. Soon I found myself at Heathrow Airport, terrified, I had never seen so many people. As for the aeroplane, it looked so small; how could it stay up in the sky? With my little suitcase, I boarded the plane and arrived in Copenhagen airport in the early hours of the morning. I was completely lost and bewildered. I had not thought of getting Danish money, and had very little sterling. One could only take £10 out of the country, that was all I had. A kindly American man saw my difficulty and insisted that I was welcome to share his taxi. Soon the taxi dropped me at the address I had been given, outside a large set of apartments. I rang the bell. There was no answer. I checked the address. After what seemed an eternity, a stern faced lady came to the door. I was in trouble again, she had no English and I had no Danish. In desperation I showed her my piece of paper with aunt and uncle's name on it. She let me in and found the correct apartment for me. I had no idea what my relations looked like, nor their ages or anything else. A small smiling man came to the door. He held out his arms and hugged me. He started to talk to me in German, then my aunt came to embrace me, again talking in German. I started to tell them, in English of course, that I spoke no German. Nothing could stop their greeting. Then uncle, who must have been at least sixty, started to speak an odd sort of English and I tried what little I had of German. Between us somehow we managed to communicate.

They were a wonderful couple and made my stay a joy. Aunt baked the most glorious coffee cake. That I do remember. I also have a vivid memory of a picnic in the middle of a wood. To my astonishment, they took all their clothes off, and very reluctantly I did the same and felt terribly embarrassed. To them, this seemed completely normal. One day Aunt Irma introduced me to a Turkish Bath. I had never heard of anything like it and thoroughly enjoyed the experience. Time flew. Soon it was time for me to return. Our goodbyes were accompanied with tears. Uncle Olaf's last words to me were 'I have learned more English from your German than I learned in school'. Although I had missed my children, I had enjoyed a week of being loved and spoiled. A year later, taking my daughter with me, I made my last visit to my relatives in Denmark. My money had run out. I do not think my husband ever forgave me for the first signs of my independence.

I saw an advertisement in the local paper for a receptionist, shorthand typist and general dogsbody. I went for an interview. At a newly opened branch of a London estate agents. The gentleman in charge was Mr. Lewis. At that time my name too was Lewis. He was some ten years younger than me and rather shy. I informed him that I had not done any shorthand and typing for some twenty years, but that I was prepared to work hard at relearning these skills. He assured me he would consider my application and would let me know after he had interviewed another ten people. I went home very despondent. What chance had I of getting this job? Had I been too honest in telling this man that I could not take dictation and type? Later that afternoon, the telephone rang. It was Mr. Lewis. He could not bear to interview any more applicants. Could I start work tomorrow?

My new job gave me great pleasure. My boss seemed pleased with my performance. My salary met my miserly requirements. We had no car any more, that had had to be sold with my business. Sid was working for the man who had taken over my business and was earning peanuts. Once again I was the wage earner. I must admit I had some good times at the Estate Agents, a very satisfying job where my talents, such as they were, were appreciated. The first time one of the owners came to the office, I was amused beyond belief. A very smart Bentley pulled up outside the office, all one could see was the top of a man's head. When this small figure came out of this smart car, I could not believe my eyes. A very small man in a very large sheepskin coat strutted into the office. I started to laugh. This was the boy whose tooth I had knocked out when we were both fifteen. He had become a millionaire, owning property all over the country. I could not stop laughing which so embarrassed my boss that he took him into the other office. I was asked to make coffee, and did so with great difficulty. All I could see was this tiny figure in his large coat.

I stayed at this office for four years by which time I had, as promised, become proficient in shorthand and typing. However, my arthritis became much worse and I could only use one hand. Our business had expanded a great deal. I had also been to one of the schools and had employed a very delightful and well qualified young girl. Now there were two of us in the office. As the business had improved beyond recognition, Mr.Lewis decided that he needed someone just as efficient as me, but with both arms. He kept insisting that I could take my time finding another job, he was not rushing me. I was absolutely shocked. I had helped build this business from nothing, now I had suddenly become inefficient despite the fact that I could run the office and him with one arm.

During the early years in this office, I had been asked to

contact all the new firms that had entered the area with a view to selling our new built houses. Ford Motor Company had opened a factory on the outskirts of Swansea. British Leyland had two factories in Llanelli. I was asked to arrange a cocktail party and invite the personnel managers from all the new factories. This I had done, very successfully. In the process I had by some freak accident been contacted by a British Leyland Transport Manager called Colin. We spoke often on the telephone but did not meet until one New Year's Eve. The rest of my life with Colin was yet to come. When I was given my marching orders, I contacted Colin. We were great friends by this time. Within two days I had found a job for myself with his help. I gave a very shocked Mr. Lewis the news that I was leaving on Friday to go to my new position on Monday and started work as a reception- ist in a large garage in a place called Fforestfach.

After two years, the Swansea branch of the company asked if they could borrow me for three weeks, they had lost their service manager. I went with pleasure, for I lived quite close to this garage. Here I stayed for four enjoyable years. I did enjoy working with men. If they saw that you knew your job, they respected you and showed it. I had always enjoyed driving and now had the opportunity to drive anything from a Mini to a Rolls Royce. It gave me great satisfaction when a customer phoned and asked for the Service Manager and paused as they realised there was a woman on the other end. I very reluctantly left this enjoyable job when I became ill.

The years passed and all my pleasure came from and through my children. They were my life and nothing I had to do for them was a hardship. I loved and was loved by my children. For that I tolerated their father. For twenty years I watched them grow up. They had their friends and thankfully felt able to bring them to our home, usually when their father was not present. I watched my beloved daughter turn from a child into a very beautiful young woman, very understanding of what went on in our house. Martin gave me the same joy as Anita had given me. As babies they were so much alike. As Martin grew older, he too became loving and as little trouble as his sister had been. Their love and affection made up for so much of the misery I had experienced and was still enduring.

Our social life was virtually non-existent. I've mentioned what happened at dances. Sid's pleasure came from visiting his mother, not my idea of enjoyment. I went as rarely as I could, then only if dad was home. Mine was an existence, not a life.

I tried desperately hard not to fight and shout in front of my children. I know I did not always succeed, and both Anita and Martin must have felt the tension. It would have been impossible for them not to have felt that their role in their father's life was not very important. He had never liked children and only tolerated his own. I cannot in all honesty remember him buying them as much as a bar of chocolate. (If I am wrong, I hope to be forgiven.) This man was the personification of selfishness. He was a hypochondriac and was only ever concerned with himself. He was never ill, but his health played a major part in his life. Ever since we first married, he had accused me of trying to poison him. And I had had to live with this stupid accusation all my married life. I don't know where he got this notion from. In fact I was a very good cook, the one thing mother had taught me. One day Anita came home from school very proud of her cooking skills. We did not, of course, eat everything, except perhaps a pudding she had cooked. We kept a Kosher home so most things were suspect if we did not know exactly what was in them. This day she noticed how tired I looked and asked me if I would like her to prepare our evening meal. I really was very tired, so of course I agreed. We sat at the table eating the meal Anita had cooked. Suddenly Sid ran from the table and went upstairs to our bedroom. I followed him to see what the matter was. He greeted me with 'your daughter is trying to poison me.' I had tolerated this stupidity when levelled at myself, but this was too much. I slapped him so hard across his face that the marks were still there next morning. How dare he say such a thing about our daughter! I really was very strong, mainly through all the physical work I had always done. I have never seen such a stunned expression on anyone's face. This was the one and only time physical violence was known in the house.

That was five years before I left him, when I could bear it no longer and had had enough. My daughter and I never discussed this state of affairs, but she was far from stupid and knew what was happening. l worked as hard as ever and went to bed each night with medication. I had been an insomniac and had to rely on medication to help me sleep. Now at last I knew that when I took my pills I would sleep without being disturbed. It was at this stage of my life that I tried committing suicide a number of times. Sid had pushed me to the very brink. When in this state I did not even consider my beloved children, I had had enough and could take no more, or so I thought. As always, God looked after me. It was not my time to die, as much as I wanted to. Now, of course, I realise these attempts were cries of help. I moved out of our bedroom and for the rest of the marriage I slept in Anita's room.

We had very few mutual friends. For me Jean was always a support and now too there was Ron. I could not have come through without their help. By this time I had got to know Colin better. Colin's marriage was as dreadful as my own. He worked too hard because he had nothing to come home to. His wife would not cook or wash for him, he did everything for himself. He had a daughter and a son whom I came to love like my own. Each evening after work Colin would come to our house for his evening meal, in fact his only meal. We came to know and like one another well. We had a great deal in common. We loved reading, in fact even liked the same books, and had a passion for waterfalls, mountains and streams. Sid and I did not possess a car at this time, so Colin would come on a Sunday to take us out to see something of the beauty we loved. Nowhere is there more beauty than in my beloved Wales. I would provide the picnic and we, including Sid, would have an enjoyable day out. On the dot of 10 o'clock Colin would go home to his lonely house. He adored his daughter, but at this time she was busy growing up and going out with boys, where before she had been daddy's girl.

Colin and I became very fond of one another and from friendship came love.

I was very fond of swimming, especially in the sea when the waves were high. I went in to swim one Sunday when the sea was especially rough. Both Colin and Sid tried hard to stop me. I enjoyed fighting with the waves and enjoyed my swim. I started to come out of the water and could not feel the right side of my upper body. Colin took me to the hospital where, after much waiting and then X-raying, I was told that I had Spondilitis. I was in great pain and went to see a specialist who informed me that it was necessary for me to have an operation to fuse two of my discs together. But when I returned to the hospital, to my dismay the specialist told me that there would be no operation. Another of my discs had disintegrated. As this was not a consecutive disc, operating was out of the question. Consequently, my right shoulder, neck and arm became paralysed. Despite not being able to use my right arm and hand and having to wear a surgical collar, I returned to work. I had to feed my children somehow. I was only thirty-five years old. The paralysis wore off, thank goodness, but the pain has rarely eased. Now at seventy-six years of age, all my discs have disintegrated and only a circle of calcium protects my neck. I still have to wear my surgical collar, especially when driving, because if I do not wear it and the car jerks suddenly, the circle of calcium will break and that will be the end of my life.

And so life continued until September 1968, just two days before Anita was about to go to college at Loughborough. For the life of me I cannot remember what happened, but a straw had broken this camel's back. Sid and I had an argument and my patience came to an end.

New Beginnings

I TALKED TO THE CHILDREN and told them what I intended to do. It was time for me to leave this miserable house. Martin was frightened. Poor lad, he really was in a quandary. I am sure he knew what had been happening between his father and me, but was too young to face that this could not go on. I packed my little car with what I thought were important things. Clothes, for I had to go to work next day, my Kenwood Mixer, the only piece of up-to-date convenience in my kitchen, and very little else. Then I drove in tears to Jean and Ron's house. I thanked God for my friends.

I rang the bell. Jean opened the door and said, 'you have done it at last, I will make up a bed.' I spent the night in tears, missing my children with a pain I could not have imagined. Next day I went to work and then to the house to see Martin and Anita. There was no problem with Anita, she understood and was ready to leave the house next day. Martin could not decide what he wanted. Yes, he wanted to be with me; no he did not want to leave what to him was security. So with a heavy heart I had to leave my beloved son with his father. I really think that this was one of the hardest things I have ever had to do.

Jean and Ron owned the house next door to theirs. It was usually let out to students. Swansea has a large overseas student population. They soon decided that I should live in the lower half of the house whilst a Pakistani lady occupied the top. We would share the bathroom and kitchen facilities. This worked very well for the moment. For a short while Sid would bring Martin to see me for an hour or so each week – the time I looked forward to so very eagerly. During the week I would pass Martin's school, usually when the school day ended, hoping to see my son. I cannot express in words how much I missed both my children. Anita had settled in to college well and was living in one of the Halls of Residence. She would phone me, so I knew she was well. How I longed for them. Each day I went to work, then back to my empty flat. No matter how I felt, I could always go next door and find love and affection and return feeling so much better.

I was still working in the garage which was situated in the Uplands, the area in which I had always lived. Sid's family also lived there, what was left of them. His mother had died some years before. I am afraid I had had no cause to mourn her. Bessie and Sadie, Sid's sisters, walked past me as if I had the plague. When my former husband remarried, he had the same treatment. Mother now lived in Bessie's house with her and my loving father-in-law. One day I received a phone call from Murray (my doctor and friend). This gentle quiet man was very upset. 'Why have you not been to the hospital, your father-in-law keeps asking for you'. I had no idea what he was talking about, no one had told me anything about him being ill. Murray knew all about his illness, his wife was a sister in the hospital and had told him of dad's distress. I immediately made time to visit the hospital the same day. On arriving at the ward, I was told that he had died during the night. I was so upset. I had loved this man dearly and felt as if I had let him down when he needed me. When no one of the family bothered to let me know of the funeral arrangements, I started to feel a deep hatred for the whole family. There was no time for me to find out the arrangements from anyone else. Jewish custom decrees that the burial take place within 24 hours of death. This harks back to the days in the desert when a body decomposes very quickly. The custom is still kept. I had no way to say my goodbyes to a man I had loved for so many years.

I often saw mother in the Uplands. The first time I saw her I approached her wanting to know how she was. She ran from me as fast as she could. Sometime later I phoned the house to speak to her. When she heard my voice, I could hear the panic in hers. All she said was 'Please do not talk to me in the street or phone me. If Bessie finds out I will have nowhere to live.' I felt very let down. I had told her five years before I left her nephew of my plans to leave him. She never accepted anything that would in any way disturb her life. In a way, I cannot blame her. She had been suffering from Parkinson's Disease for many years, now there was no way she could live alone, so had to rely on her niece. Although I understood her reasons, I could not but be hurt by her attitude. We had become very close since my marriage and now I was once more being rejected. Shortly after this rejection I heard via my solicitor, that mother had gone into a Jewish Old Age Home in Cardiff. I wanted to visit her but Colin would not allow me to even contact her. He had seen my hurt when she rejected me and there was no way he would allow this to be repeated. She died two years later, aged ninety-three. I did not hear about her death for six months, and then it was by pure chance. I met a member of the Jewish Congregation. I admit, I had avoided any such meeting, I was afraid of once more being rejected. But I was wrong, I started to meet more and more of my friends and the last thing on their minds was rejection. It was only then I learned that despite my efforts to keep my dreadful marriage secret, people are not stupid and had seen how miserable I was and had been for a long time. And they did not blame me, they blamed Sid.

Time passed slowly. Each day was like the one before, lonely. Home was an empty flat. I did not even have Sundays to look forward to. Sid had by this time refused to bring Martin and it was too far for him to come on his own. My misery was only eased by Colin. He came each day after work. We would eat together and chat until on the dot of 10 he would leave me and go home to his own empty room.

In December I became very ill. Our doctor came daily but could not find out what was the matter. The poor man tried everything, but nothing stopped my illness from becoming worse. One Saturday afternoon the doorbell rang. Colin went to the door, opened it and Martin stood there in the rain looking like a drowned and very miserable boy. He threw himself on to the bed and cried like a baby. As I looked at him I was horrified. His coat was in rags, his shoes had holes in them, he looked like a tramp. He had begun to grow and had become alarmingly tall.

Unfortunately, he had developed trouble with the muscles behind his knees. It appeared that he had suffered from malnutrition. As a growing boy this had affected his cartilages which had all but disintegrated. He was in great pain and had to attend the hospital regularly. After all these years, he still suffers pain from this neglect.

Unfortunately, my illness was getting worse and worse. Despite this, I was happy. I had my dear son with me. Jean looked after my needs when Colin was at work. However, Murray, our doctor, in sheer desperation called a gynaecologist to see me. She examined me and within an hour I was on the operating table. She had found that my uterus was filled with fibroids. The only answer was a hysterectomy. In those days it meant two weeks in hospital and three months off work. Despite everything, we had a wonderful Christmas. I had both my children about me; Colin was there as were Jean and Ron. We wanted for nothing. I was surrounded by all those I loved. Anita slept in Martin's bed and Martin slept on the sofa, his legs hanging over the end. Despite still being horribly ill, it was one of my happiest times. Soon after Christmas, Jean too had to go into hospital for the same operation that I had undergone not long before. Still we coped. Nothing could dim my happiness. Anita looked after the two of us, Jean and myself whilst she was on vacation from Loughborough. Afterwards we managed somehow, but we always managed. It seemed as if, now that I had my children and Colin, Jean and Ron, nothing else mattered.

I think it was the happiness we shared, our complete contentment that made Colin decide it was time to leave his miserable house and for us to start a life together. Colin's children had both married by this time and this was all he had been waiting for. I spent hours on the telephone and, when better, called at every estate agent and letting agency. Eventually we found a small two-bedroom house to let but as regards furniture we had nothing except Colin's own bed. After a search in the local paper for second or third hand furniture, we found a sofa bed, which was made of solid iron and almost immovable. Friends gave us things they had no further use for. We took everything gratefully. We really did not care. We were content to have a roof over our heads. Eventually we had an almost furnished house. Our kitchen/dining room was furnished from the canteen of the firm Colin worked for. They supplied all the cutlery and crockery too.

Although Sid had always said he would never divorce me, we did not much care about that, we were happy. I had to return to work, but the garage was out of the question. The doctors were adamant that it would be foolish to subject my arthritis to so much cold. Within a short while I found a job as a receptionist in a garage, doing work that I loved. We had to have money. Colin's wife still lived in his original home and all expenses for her and the house had to be paid for. Unfortunately one wage earner was not enough. We both worked hard but we were happy.

Eventually Sid decided to divorce me. Even during the time we were married, he had been teaching an old friend of ours to drive. Anita and I found this hysterical. He was an atrocious driver and we felt sorry for his pupil. Still, he found her more amenable than I had been and decided to marry her.

Jean went with me to court. We sat there stunned as the cause of the divorce was read out; 'mental cruelty.' Sid had a psychiatrist with him who told the court that because I had not shared his bed for five years, this had affected his health. We did not know where to look. What sort of man would stand up in court and waffle about how badly treated he had been by his wife? Only then, after twenty years, did I discover that even before we had married, he had been receiving psychiatric treatment. I always suspected the man was mad. I was not so pleased when I had to pay his as well as my costs. Sid had sold the house and I was left with the princely sum of £1,500 after all the expenses were paid. This I swore I would never touch; it was all I had to leave to my children.

I was free and nothing else mattered. Now we had the problem of Colin's divorce. His wife was another person who swore never to divorce him. We bided our time. After a year or so, we discovered that Colin's wife had been going on holiday and was seeing a man friend on an on and off basis. Eventually this turned into a serious relationship and a divorce and remarriage. We were so anxious to see her married that Anita and I sat with scarves over our heads outside the registry office to make sure that the marriage went ahead. Within days of this marriage, Colin and I put up the banns for our own wedding. Colin's mother had never approved of us living together without being married. Each time he would phone her asking her to visit us, she would put the phone down. We had in our ignorance, thought that this was because, being extremely deaf, she wore hearing aids in both ears and could not hear him. When we had set the date for our wedding, he again phoned his mother asking her to come to our wedding. After many excuses, she came with friends of Colin who picked her up at her house and brought her to the Registry Office. Colin's son Paul was his best man, Martin gave me away and Anita was my bridesmaid. There was no one in the world I would have changed places with. Happiness at last. To add to my joy, I had acquired another son in Paul who, never judging us, had supported us during all the years we had been together. I had come to love him as I loved my own children. He became part of my family and I hope he will always stay so.

Mother was so delighted with our wedding and reception she decided to come with us on our honeymoon in Devon where we had been given the loan of a caravan as a wedding gift. A good time was had by all. Colin and I laughed almost the whole two weeks. Mother in her wisdom, would remove both her hearing aids, then call Colin to put out her light. Thus thinking she was giving us privacy. She forgot that we had lived together for some years, but thought this was our honeymoon. In the few years that mother lived, she came to us almost every few weeks. The telephone would ring, 'Colin come and pick me up I am coming to spend a few days with you.' I loved her very much and she came to love me for which I am very grateful. I only wish we could have had her for longer.

Time went by, we still lived in our little house. Martin was now working in transport, as he did not know what he wanted to do. Anita, my very beautiful daughter, brought home Hugh and they had their engagement celebration in our little home. The one thing mother always wanted was for us to move back into Colin's house in Pennard. Unfortunately, she did not live long enough to see this, but move back we did. When the opportunity arose, Colin asked me whether I wanted him to sell the house he had shared with his former wife and purchase a new home for us. I loved the area so much and was determined that I would make this house very different to its former condition. We were able to do this thanks to mother, who left enough in her will enabling us to pay Colin's former wife for her half of the house she had neglected so badly. This was the law and we were pleased not to be in her debt.

Three years later Anita and Hugh married in Lychfield. The wedding was supposed to take place in Swansea. All the arrangements had been made but these had to be changed as the couple had found a house they wanted to buy. So it was decided to cancel the Swansea plans and marry in Lychfield. As Hugh was a Methodist, Anita decided to give up her Jewish faith and join Hugh and become a Methodist. Colin was so proud, walking Anita his beloved daughter (neither Colin nor I were comfortable with the 'step' word and never used it) down the aisle. The wedding went wonderfully well and Anita looked very beautiful. I was so proud of her and was filled with love for all my family. We travelled from Swansea in a convoy of five cars, so many family and friends wanting to be at the wedding, a journey all thought well worthwhile making.

Finding Papa

IT WAS 1980 and plans were going ahead for Martin and Wendy's marriage in June. Early in the year, an article appeared in our local evening paper which read as follows; 'Anyone knowing the whereabouts of Ellen Kerry Lewis (my first married name) please contact J. Wertheim' – at an address in Melbourne, Australia. As Papa's name was Julius, I jumped to the conclusion that he must be very ill or dying and wanted to contact me. I was wrong. We managed to find the telephone number in Australia. As there is an 11-hour time difference, Colin and I stayed up alternate nights to telephone. Each time there was no answer. A week later, a friend came to tea. I said to her 'If this darned article is in again today I will phone regardless of time'. When it was there again, I picked up the telephone and dialled the number I already knew by heart. A very sleepy female Australian voice started to swear at me. Started to tell me that it was 3 a.m. and that she was tired having just returned from holiday. When I managed to get a word in, I told her that I had been phoning for a week without any joy, and asked what the matter was with Papa. This lady suddenly realised who I was. Surprised that her advertisement had been answered so quickly and full of apologies, she told me that Papa had died four years before and she was his widow. After this conversation, we started to correspond. She wanted us to go to Australia. Of course, I immediately wanted her to come to Britain for Martin and Wendy's wedding. She said that she had high blood pressure and her doctor would not allow her to make such a long journey. We continued to correspond, her letters were very affectionate and, it was clear, she really wanted us to visit her very badly.

In letter after letter she became more persistent. We would only have to pay our fares. She, Jeanne, had no accommodation, but her friend Greta had a spare bedroom. We would have the use of Papa's car, plus this and that. It was all very persuasive. Colin had just been made redundant from his firm which had been a great shock though really not unexpected.

We put off our decision until after Martin's wedding – a day of great happiness. Wendy looked beautiful. Martin had become a wonderful man. I felt very proud. He was six feet tall and handsome. Paul acted as his best man. A choice that gave us all great pleasure, though none of us knew of it until the day of the wedding. The day was complete for me. Not only did I have all three of my children there, but also Daniel, my grandson.

The time had come to make our decision regarding our trip to Australia. Colin was all for going, he loved to travel. I, as always, was the one who was concerned over finances. Colin, as I have said, had been made redundant, and his world fell apart. He had always been in charge and had a wonderful brain. Having joined the army at nineteen, by twenty-five he had risen to the rank of Major, having spent four years in India. Back in the U.K., he went to university during the day and drove lorries at night. Eventually, he had enough qualifications to find a job as Transport Manager with a firm in Birmingham. Later he moved to a firm called Pressed Steel Fisher which later still changed its name to British Leyland. Eventually he was sent to South Wales to take charge of transport at their new factory at Llanelli. After many years the firm reorganised, combining different departments. One of these involved transport. It was decided that Colin's position could be incorporated with another. I think all this broke Colin's heart. He was never the same. He had lost what, other than his family, he loved most. There was no salary coming in. Colin was only sixty-three, so for two years we would have to manage until his pension came at sixty-five. Of course, I too wanted to go to Australia. Wanted to know why this unknown widow of Papa's wanted to see us so badly.

December, 1981, after a stopover in Bangkok, we arrived in Melbourne to a great reception. There were bunches of flowers, baskets of fruit, some from Jeanne, my stepmother – what a strange word to use at my age. Some of the gifts were from her friends, delightful people. We were taken to Greta's home to meet her and put our luggage away. She was a wonderful lady;

no one could have made us more welcome. A widow who lived alone, she had a lovely Scottish accent. The more we came to know her the more we came to love her.

Jeanne was an attractive looking lady, but rather temperamental. She lived in what we would call a bungalow but they called a unit which she had shared with Papa for the four years they had been married. We walked to her home each day, some three miles. The temperature was in the 100's and my arthritis was giving me trouble. Papa's car was rarely at our disposal; there was always some excuse. We went with Jeanne to shop then back to the house for a meal and sat in her six foot of garden for the rest of the day, and so home to Greta's, where at last we could relax. Whilst with Jeanne, we saw nothing of Melbourne, for she lived in the suburbs, a place called Moorrabbin. We met some of her brothers and sisters. And we had Christmas lunch on the beach. During the rest of the holidays the brothers and their wives invited us to many barbecues. Colin and I thoroughly enjoyed the outdoor life. They were a wonderful gang and great fun and very affectionate.

After the holidays we went back to the old routine. To Jeanne's for lunch, then the garden for a while in the afternoon. Then back to Greta's. During this time something happened or was said between Jeanne and Greta. Their long friendship came to an abrupt end. We didn't even know what caused this rift, but we didn't think it had to do with Colin and me. After three weeks, Jeanne told us that the doctor had insisted that she stopped all this gadding about, so would only see us once or twice a week. At her insistence we had booked this trip to last four and a half months. Here we were after a few weeks being rejected for reasons we could not understand. In all the time we had spent with Jeanne, we had never had a cross word. When I told her that I did not know if, when she wanted to see us, I would be well enough to do the long trek to her home, she rejected us completely, would not even speak to us. We were now in an invidious position. Staying with someone who was no longer a friend of my stepmother. We felt very awkward. I spoke to Greta. And told her we would try to find alternative accommodation. At this she became very upset, she had become as fond of us as we of her. So on condition that we would pay for our meals etc., we stayed.

Next day we went out and bought ourselves a very ancient car. There was no way we could manage to get about for nearly four months without transport. When Jeanne's family found out what had happened, they became very upset and took us under their collective wing. The boys stripped the car to make sure it was road-worthy, the girls found seat covers to absorb the heat. When the car was in tiptop condition, Colin and I were allowed to drive it. The parties continued. We were happier with these friends than we had been with Jeanne. We travelled around some of Australia and had a wonderful time and made many friends. During the early days of our estrangement from Jeanne, Greta, who had known Papa for many years, asked me to go to Melbourne and visit the probate office. It appeared that she had always had reservations regarding something Jeanne had done during one of Papa's heart attacks. I did not want anything to do with this request. Greta insisted that this was for my own good. I had not come to Australia to scrounge money or anything else that did not belong to me. I hadn't known that Papa had made a success of his business and might have money or property to leave. I just was not interested in material things. I wanted to find out why Papa had rejected me all these years. But we went to the probate office and requested a copy of Papa's will. To my utter amazement, I discovered that not only had he remembered me, but also named both my children. The will stated that Jeanne was to have the interest accrued by his investments. The capital and property were to be divided, half to me, the other half divided between Anita and Martin. I was deeply affected. All I could think of was that Papa had not forgotten me or my children. The money meant nothing to me. It would be nice to have but the important part of this will was that we had been remembered.

This will had been lodged when he married Jeanne. I contacted the solicitor, now long retired, who had written it and although he did not live in Melbourne, he agreed to meet me at his old office which was still working. He greeted me with much affection. He had not only been my Papa's solicitor, but also his friend. The poor man was almost in tears as he explained to me that the will of which I had a copy was 'null and void'. During one of Papa's heart attacks, Jeanne had found another solicitor and had Papa sign a document that put all he owned into joint names. Hence, this will was not worth the paper it was written on. It may sound very strange, but I was not the least bit upset. The only thing that mattered to me, was that we had been remembered by Papa. What a shame he had rejected me all those years ago. I met a number of Papa's friends who had come to Australia with him on the Dunera. They told me a great deal about Papa's life. His happy, but childless marriage to his second wife. His hard work making his business a success. These men made Papa real to me after so many lonely years. They told me that my father had spoken about me, not often, just occasionally. They were under the impression that I lived in London. He never told his friends why he had not contacted me over these many years. My Papa the extrovert, had become a private person; some subjects were not for discussion and I was one of them. They were very surprised when I spoke about my siblings and how they had died with Mutti. Papa had only ever mentioned me. His friends had thought that I was the only child he had. I was told that my wedding photograph lived on top of his sideboard from which it was never moved. Jeanne had given me a very tattered little photograph Papa had kept in his wallet for fiftyplus years. The photograph was a copy of the original which was sent to Swansea in 1939. I still have and treasure this little photograph because my Papa had always kept it with him. Our visit to Australia had become well worth making, if only for the information I discovered about Papa. No-one knew why he had rejected me for all those years, now I too stopped worrying about this subject. Papa had died in 1976. May he rest in peace.

All things must come to an end and we returned to Swansea after a wonderful holiday. Things were not easy. Colin was used to going to work and it irked him to be idle. During our stay in Australia the boys had taught him to play golf. This now together with his hobby of stamp collecting filled his days. I had been for many years a member of the WRVS, cooking for luncheon clubs and helping run the canteen in our local prison. So I too kept busy.

Part Three
Rediscovery

Rediscovery

ALL MY LIFE, like all Jewish people, I wanted to visit Israel. Unlike most I had a motive besides just sightseeing. I very much wanted to go to Yad Vashem, the Holocaust Museum. There I knew was a library of millions of people lost in the Holocaust. I hoped and prayed that I would find some information about what had really happened to my family. I could not face doing this alone, so asked Anne a friend I made during the tour, to come with me. She managed to see just one of the rooms. Not being able to bear the rest, she ran crying outside where she found a bench on which to sit. I felt I had to see all the heartwrenching sights so went from room to room not really seeing much for my tears blinded me. When I finished breaking my heart, I went to the building where the millions of records were kept. Here, a very caring man took me around without success. Nowhere could we find the name of Wertheim. My kindly companion assured me that he would continue the search after I returned home and would be in touch. Before leaving, he insisted on giving me the name of a tracing agency in Germany. He insisted that on my arrival in Swansea I write to this agency in case they had further information.

Some weeks after my return, I received a letter from the helpful man I had met at Yad Vashem. He had continued, as promised, to search the files. On the corner of a letter he had come across the name Wertheim. This letter was from a lady who had visited the Records Office ten years before me and lived in New York. The span of ten years made me reluctant to approach her, for in my imagination she must by now be either very old or deceased. His letter was full of sympathy. This man, too, had come to the conclusion that my family had died and no records named them. Nevertheless, I felt that the visit to Israel, despite the disappointment, had been a success and I felt better for having realised an ambition long felt.

Suddenly, after many months I received a copy of the letter I had been sent by the German Red Cross when I was thirteen years old. I could not face the contents at thirteen and at fifty-eight it was much more difficult. I collapsed and our doctor kept me sedated for a little while. The next memory was waking up to find Colin sitting on my bed, a cup of tea in one hand and an airmail letter in the other. 'Drink your tea and write to New York,' were his first words. Pulling myself together and desperately trying to stop crying, I did as Colin asked. A few weeks passed and I received another letter from New York, from the wife of my father's third cousin. His name was Maurice and he had two sisters and two brothers all living in New York. We corresponded for a while and I decided I was going to meet my nearest relative, even if he was just a third cousin.

When I made my intentions known to my American family, I received many letters, some letting me know that they had no accommodation for me. Being very blasè and having no idea what awaited me in America, I flew to Kennedy Airport. It was a terrifying place. The whole world seemed to be in this enor-mous airport. Taking my courage in both hands I found a taxi and gave the driver the address. A long drive later, I found myself outside a large block of not very smart apartments, rang the bell and was greeted warmly by the cousins. Martha, Maurice's wife, kept telling me that they had nowhere for me to sleep. I could see this, but was not worried. I was sure I could find accommoda-tion for myself. We had hardly finished the meal they had prepared when the telephone started to ring. It was Maurice's brothers and sisters. I did not know what to say to them until I realised they were not interested in me as such, but more because I was my father's daughter. It appeared that they had all adored my father. He was the wicked boy, always in mischief, whom they would have loved to have been, had they had the courage. Maurice gave me a photograph of the class in school which included him, his sister Ellen and my Papa. All the children looked neat and tidy, bar one. He looked as if he had been dragged through a hedge backwards and had a 'never do care' look. Of course, it was Papa.

Phone calls kept coming, I was getting more and more tired and wished they would stop. Quite late in the evening, a call came from a lady who kept shouting at me 'You must come to Los Angeles, I am your second cousin.' She repeated this time and time again. When I managed to get a word in, I told her I had only just arrived and could not contemplate a visit to L.A. From what I had by now been told, I doubted if I had enough money to keep me in New York for two weeks. But Toni, that was her name, still kept on shouting. Eventually she put Alex, her husband on the phone; he asked me if I had a pen and paper and told me to write down a dozen or so numbers which he told me was his American Express number. He suggested that I stay in N.Y. for a week, but then I was to book a flight to L.A. using his American Express card number. I was very weary by this time and slept on the sofa. Next day I went into New York and with great difficulty found myself a small, cheap hotel.

I spent a wonderful week in New York, doing all the things women on their own shouldn't do. Like travelling on the subway at night alone. Each evening I went to Astoria where the family lived and had a meal with them. Each evening Maurice would insist that I take a taxi back to my hotel. But after two evenings unable to afford any more taxi fares I took the subway. On all these trips, I never felt fear, nor was I ever accosted. The only rude people I found in the States were the policemen. I loved New York and vowed to return.

The day before my flight to L.A. I spent with Ellen. We enjoyed each other's company even though there was a large age gap between us. Even as a child, I never found difficulty in enjoying older people's company. Perhaps this was because I have never truly been a child, but always a small grown up. Sunday I flew to Los Angeles. Not knowing the people I was going to meet, I had telephoned them in advance to inform them what I was wearing, so they would at least recognise me. I waited and waited at the airport, when suddenly, I couldn't believe my eyes. It was like looking into a mirror twenty years on. Toni and I looked so alike. Our hair, complexion, even the way we walked.

I had always been taught to walk very upright and still do so to this day. The likeness between Toni and me was uncanny. Yes, she was twenty years older, but other than that we could have been sisters. They took me to their wonderful house on a mountain. It really was very beautiful. Jack their son, an architect, had designed it to Toni's specification. With a pair of Mercedes in the garage, they wanted for nothing. Despite their wealth, they were the most down to earth people one could meet. I loved them from day one and felt that this was reciprocated. As Toni made the tea, with her back turned to me, she asked me whether I had been in touch with my Uncle David who was she said my father's eldest brother. I had never heard of him, at least by that name. My grandmother Selma, Papa's mother, had taken her six sons and one daughter to America in the Thirties, perhaps 1936 or 7. This Uncle's name was Fritz, but in the States he had called himself David. Then she asked me about Erika. Yes, Erika I knew, or rather knew about. She was my Papa's youngest sister and only two years older than me. I had always had to wear her discarded clothes. Erika, it seemed was in Miami. Leaving the kettle, she picked up the telephone and the next thing I knew someone was shouting at me again, 'When are you coming', over and over. I managed to get a word in and explained I had just arrived and had to return to Britain in a week's time. He still wanted to know when I was coming? Knowing that my uncle had to be in his eighties, I promised I would try to return the following year to see him. Toni and Alex gave me a wonderful week. To our delight, we three enjoyed the same things, music, art, and all things that brought us joy.

I returned home to Swansea, full of my new family and of the joy they had brought me. I had made up my mind that in the future I would return to the U.S. to see Uncle David, his wife Sally and Erika and her husband Larry. Before making all these plans, Erika and I started to correspond. In one of her letters, she asked me if I knew I had cousins in Cincinnati. It seems that when Opa and Oma went to South America, they took with them one of my Papa's brothers; he then married my Mutti's sister. These cousins were in fact double cousins. They could not make a living in Argentina, so had come to the U.S. and settled in Cincinnati. Erika gave me the male cousin's address and I wrote to him. A week later, I had a call from Sal from Cincinnati. He went on to tell me that he had been in touch with Erika and had sent tickets for me to fly to Cincinnati and stay for four days. He and his wife were celebrating their Silver Wedding and wanted me to be with them.

In Cincinnati I was met by about a dozen people. One holding up a card on a stick on which the name Kerry appeared in large letters. Then I was being hugged by many arms. I looked up and could not believe my eyes; once more I was seeing an image of myself but this time much younger. She was Juanita, the female cousin, and again my double cousin. Eventually, we arrived at Sal's home where his wife immediately put on a kettle. There must be something about me that silently asks for tea. Kettles are automatically put on for me and tea made. This time it was American tea, a teabag dipped into hot water, not our British tea. While we were talking, the door flew open and a lady dashed into the room. She hugged me saying, 'You do not remember me?' During my life I had had a name in my head, the name of Sonja. I never knew who this was, now I found out. This was Sonja. She was four years younger than me. The last time we had met, she must have been about three. As an only child, she loved to come to see us; we were such a crowd. I had treated her the way I treated my brothers and sisters, with love. She had always remembered this. Her father was Mutti`s brother. Another cousin. Sunny, as she was now known, had lost her husband about three weeks before I came to the States, so had not come to the party.

My cousins were now mounting up. Erika had a son, whom I met in Miami, a daughter I did not meet, plus the three in Cincinnati. The evening of the party came and it was very confusing. As Sal and his wife came from Argentina, they had many friends from there, so they spoke Spanish, while other guests spoke German and I spoke only English. How confusing can things become? I was soon to find out. A man came up to me and asked me if I was Sal's cousin? Of course I said I was. He wanted to know on which side. Both sides. Then we too are related. I asked him how? 'My grandfather and your grandmother were brother and sister' – so even more relations. From none, my family was growing bigger and bigger.

Four days later, I was back in Miami. Staying with Erika and Larry. I saw Uncle David and Aunt Sally almost each day. It hurt to see my uncle; he looked so like Papa. Three days afterwards, I was on another plane going to see Toni and Alex for a further week. Another wonderful week, then home again. My stories by this time were stranger than fiction and I had at last found what I call my 'birth family'. Felt much loved and loved them all in return.

Over the years I visited the States often. Mostly in the winter, plane fares are much cheaper. Sunny and I have become very close over the years. Each visit to the States I stay with her in Cincinnati. We have a great deal in common and enjoy one another's company. We do not have to continually talk. We find enjoyment in just being together. We can sit in two rooms reading books, (we even enjoy the same books) and still find companionship. I do not appreciate American TV which Sunny enjoys. She sits on her enormous bed and watches things that interest her, whilst I sit in the family room either reading a book or watching videos we borrow from the local library. At home I rarely go to the cinema, so when with Sunny, I catch up on films I have missed. Sunny has three children, two girls and a boy and four grandsons. I love them all very much and feel they return my affection. It is always the highlight of my year when I visit Sunny and her family. For me Cincinnati is a place in which I can relax, enjoy being loved and spoiled, it has a very special place in my heart.

Opa Herman Kaiser (b. 1877), Oma Emilia Kaiser (b. 1880),
Johanna (my mother, b. 1905), Siegfried (b. 1907), Max (b. 1910),
Alma (b. 1912), Alfred (b. 1914), David (b. 1915), Leo (b. 1909).

Mother holding Ludwig; Papa holding Ruth;
below her Sally; Rolf, Heinz and me, 1937.

Passport giving me permission to land at Southampton.

Document permitting me to enter the United Kingdom,
ostensibly 'for educational purposes', in reality, to save my life.

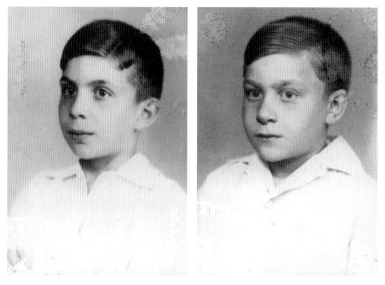

My brothers Rolf (b. 1930) and Heinz (b. 1931),
photographed in 1940.

Werner and Horst Golnik, who were on the transport
to Riga with my family and saw them being shot.

My American family in 1985 (from top): Uncle David and Aunt Sally;
with my Aunt Erika in Miami; Cousin Sal (left) at a welcoming
party in Cincinnati; and Cousins Juanita and Sonja (Sunny);
Second Cousin Toni in L.A.; Sunny and I in 1996.

My Great Grandmother Sprinz Kaiser's grave in Hoof.

Burial place and memorial, Riga-Bikernieki,
which I visited in late December 2001.

Clark's College, Swansea, Session 1942–43. I'm seated, far right.

Colin and I on our first holiday together in Spain, 1970.

1999, joint celebration for my 70th and Colin's 80th birthday (January 9th and 21st respectively).

Jean, my dearest friend and a great support.

Martin, Anita and me, 2000.

Martin and his wife, Wendy.

Anita, Hugh and their children Hannah and Daniel.

Colin's son Paul is a second son to me. Here he is pictured with wife Eira and son Jack. Edward and Alex complete the family.

Reunion

EARLY IN 1989 I was told by friends that they had heard a lady by the name of Bertha Leverson speak on the radio about a plan for a 50th anniversary Kindertransport Reunion. I too started listening to the radio and sometime later heard these plans for myself. She was asking people, who had come over on the Kindertransports between 1938 and 1939, to contact her to see how many would actually attend such an occasion. Prior to hearing this I had never clearly thought about others like myself who had come as refugees to Britain. The plans for the reunion went ahead and I found myself in London going to a two-day reunion of people I had never met. It was an unbelievable experience. I later discovered that 970 people from many countries had taken part.

As I arrived, having travelled on a special bus full of strangers, I began a conversation with a very shy lady who had come from Israel. Neither of us knew what to expect and neither of us thought that we would know another soul at the reunion. At the beginning we stayed together. I have never felt such emotion, generated by people who, like us, had arrived not knowing anyone else. But occasionally strangers would look at one another and recognise a friend they had not seen for fifty years. The screams of joy and the tears of happiness were overwhelming. This reunion of strangers kept happening over and over again. I stood there feeling very alone for I hadn't met anyone I could recognise. When I had arrived in the UK, I had gone straight to Swansea, which for the purpose of meeting others like myself was in the middle of nowhere.

We were greeted at the entrance with labels. Each one stating our names, the date on which we had arrived and the town from which we had come. (It was just like that original arrival.) On each table in this enormous hall were names of towns from which children like me had come. When I found the table with Kassel on it, there were only two other ladies there. We introduced ourselves: Henny, some four years older than I; Dorrith, two years younger. They both had their husbands with them, both husbands, like mine, non-Jewish. I felt very alone, but knew that Colin would not have been interested. We started to chat. Unfortunately, I had no photographs or memorabilia from Germany, so had nothing to show them. Suddenly Dorrith took out a photograph album from a small case. Being older than her, I could not imagine that these school pictures would have anything to do with me. She insisted I looked. In one of the school photographs, I recognised a familiar face. I thought my heart had stopped. Amongst other children there was a picture of Heinz, the brother who had been two years my junior and therefore nearer Dorrith's age. I could not contain myself and burst into tears.

Henny, too, had photographs which we looked through, but found nothing further to touch me. Her photographs were mainly of her family. Henny had been lucky, she had come with her sister. I thought this was wonderful; to have another person with you was, as far as I was concerned, heaven. Dorrith had gone to a non-Jewish family in Scotland where she had had a good childhood. She was also lucky enough to have had grandparents who had managed to get to Canada. This must have been wonderful. Although she was brought up in a Christian household, she was always conscious of the fact that she was Jewish. Of course, my grandparents had been in Argentina, where I had corresponded with them, but not very satisfactorily for they wrote in German and I replied in English. I had managed to make out the gist of their letters, and had even received two photographs of Opa and Oma. Oma, by this time, had died some years before. I had so wanted to see them just once. I rather envied both Dorrith and Henny. They had something to show from their past and I nothing. We three became friends immediately. They had both returned to Kassel, something I didn't feel I could do. Henny still had an aunt living there, a very old lady, who had thankfully survived. Henny had visited her a number of times. Dorrith and her husband had returned to

Kassel a number of times. Now they promised to return to Germany and try to find out if anyone knew what had happened to my family.

The reunion lasted two days. On the second day there was a symposium, consisting of local teachers asking questions of a panel made up from people from the Kindertransport. If the audience wished, they too could answer some of the questions. After a number of questions and answers, one of the teachers asked what we of the Kindertransport now felt was our homeland? Answers came thick and fast. To my dismay a number of people in the audience answered that despite all the things they had gone through and their allegiance to Britain or wherever they now lived (I haven't mentioned that the Kinder came to the reunion from all over the world, one man even came from Peru), they still felt that their homeland was Germany. Without knowing what I was doing, I left my seat and walked to the stage. I cannot remember ever being so angry. When it became my turn to speak, I was told I spoke with great passion. I told the audience that I was disgusted with these answers. I was myself a wife, mother and grandmother. That this country, despite my foster mother, had been very good to me. I was Jewish and proud of it. But what I did not feel was any affinity for Germany. How could I? Germany had robbed me of a mother, four brothers and two sisters. I was British and proud of it. I wanted nothing to do with Germany. I was amazed at myself. There were some 970 people in the hall. I was truly shy, yet I had stood in front of this audience and had spoken from my heart. As I came off the stage, the room erupted. People were fighting their way to me, they hugged, kissed me and everyone told me that I had spoken the words that they had in their hearts yet couldn't find the ability to speak. It had become sheer chaos. I was very touched and in tears. People I had never met would not let me go back to my seat, all they wanted was to touch or kiss me to release their emotion at hearing the words they could not speak and I had spoken for them. When at last the hall became calm once more and I tried to return to my seat, I was stopped by a young woman with a microphone and a recorder. She told me she was from the BBC and wanted to interview me for *Woman's Hour*. I agreed to be interviewed. Because of the noise in the hall, we decided to walk some distance away. When we had finished the young lady was in tears. She told me how desperately she wanted the full interview to be broadcast, but unfortunately there would not be nearly enough time. When the interview was broadcast only about ten minutes of air time was available.

Dorrith and her husband returned to Kassel for me. Then visited me in Swansea with a very large memorial book printed in Kassel. It named all the Jewish people who had lived in the town and in nearby villages before the war. I even found my own name. The Wertheim family had a full page to themselves. There were even photographs of Rolf and Heinz, my two brothers. According to this book, my whole family had perished. I so desperately needed to have this confirmed but could not bring myself to return to Germany.

Something else had happened at the reunion. A programme had been printed with the names and addresses of the people taking part. Another part of the programme contained names of the Kinder who wanted to take part but could not for many reasons: distance, lack of money, even lack of space in this enormous hall. I did not read this part of the programme until I returned home. One evening, looking through the list of those who couldn't take part, I came across the name and address of my great friend, the only one I had been able to turn to many, many years earlier. When I read his address in Moorrabin, Melbourne, Australia, I could not believe my eyes. When Colin and I had gone to Australia, we had actually stayed for four months just around the corner from him. Each day we went out, we passed a Synagogue. Each Saturday, I was tempted to enter, but never did. What a shame. We could have met so many years before. Now I told Colin that I must get in touch with him immediately. But before I had time to write, having seen my name and address in the programme, he had immediately written to me. I told him how torn I was about Germany. I had another disadvantage, I could no longer speak German. I had tried to learn it in night school but found I had developed a psychological block. It's true I could read and understand a little, but there was no way I could speak it. The other reason of course was that I had not spoken German since I was ten years old.

After a while I received a letter from my old friend telling me that he was coming to the UK for a holiday and to see friends he had not seen for many years. Financially it was not feasible for him to come very often. The letter went on to say that he too needed to go back to Hamburg, his home town, in the hope of finding out what had happened to his father. At last I had a companion who would give me all the support I needed.

Journey to the Past

OUR JOURNEY to our past took place in June 1992. We met at Heathrow Airport. Despite having exchanged photographs, his first words to me were, 'Your hair is grey.' I answered, 'You have very little hair yourself.' What a meeting. We had not seen one another for nearly thirty-five years, yet within minutes it was as if we had never been apart. We spent four days in Hamburg. Wonderful days. This beautiful city held no memories for me, good or bad. I had never been there before. We visited his old home, and the site of the Hebrew school, which he had attended in his youth. Being some seven years older than me, and living in a large city, his memories were not as painful as mine were of Kassel. We spent the days sightseeing. We both loved the harbour and ships. We took a boat that went around the harbour and another day took another boat farther a field. I enjoyed eating fresh fish that tasted as if it had just jumped out of the sea.

During these four days we never stopped talking. There was so much to catch up on. How our lives had changed. We spoke of the old days when he was in Swansea. For the first time we spoke of our feelings for one another. I asked why he had not spoken of these when I needed to know that he cared. How miserable I had been, loving him and his non reciprocation. Only then did he tell me a truth I had never imagined. He had not left Swansea for a more lucrative job. Mother had threatened him. If he did not go away, she told him she would inform the synagogue authorities of his supposed unbecoming behaviour towards a young woman. He a married man with two children could not take the chance that mother would carry out her threat. I knew that she would have done exactly as she threatened. Once again, mother had cost me years of happiness. He went on to tell me that some years before, when his life too had been unbearable, he had asked his wife for a divorce (this was long before we met). His father-in-law, (who had been his sponsor when he came to this country in 1938), had threatened him with similar threats, although he had done nothing wrong, except be miserable enough to leave his wife and child. It seemed we would never stop talking, there was so much to say after so many silent years.

The time came to travel to Kassel. I had been in touch with a friend of Dorrith's called Esther Hass. Dorrith had met her on one of her trips to Kassel. We phoned her from Hamburg and arranged to meet her the next evening at our Kassel Hotel. Esther was a very shy lady. She could speak a little English but was too self-conscious to even try. We took her out for a meal and asked about the buses or trains to Hoof, now called Shonenberg. There were buses, but they ran only about twice a day. As for trains, it was as I had remembered, no station, no train. Esther insisted that we borrow her car, as she was not using it next day. We said that we would prefer to hire a car but she would not hear of it. She arrived next day in her rather old Ford. Now we were in a quandary. My careful friend had left all his papers in the hotel safe in Hamburg so had no driving licence. I had my licence but had never driven a left-hand drive car, added to which I had been driving an automatic car. Owing to my arthritis, I had weakness in both my right arm and leg. Now I was faced with driving a borrowed car, something I hate doing, the gears were on the wrong side and I was very, very nervous. Esther left the car and us on the side of the main road to Hoof. My poor friend had never driven with me before and was almost as nervous as I. My one vanity has always been my good driving, now it proved itself. I had driven about half way when he said 'Why are you nervous? You are a good driver'. This cheered me a mile. We arrived in Hoof, unfortunately too early for the Town Hall to be open. While waiting, I realised this building was very familiar. In fact it was my old school.

Eventually we went in and asked the lady at the enquiry desk where we could find the information we required. She told us she knew a man who could help and directed us to a Herr Schunder. It seems that when he and two friends retired, they set themselves the task of writing the history of the Jewish people of

Hessen, the name of the main area, once one of the small states before it became Germany. We drove to his house, but not before we found ourselves in some trouble. I could drive straight but using the gears with my weak arm was becoming difficult. So we compromised, I depressed the clutch whilst my friend changed gear. Had I not been so unbearably miserable, it would have been funny.

When we found Herr Schunder, he was very helpful. Dorrith, on her previous visit to Hoof, had brought back the story of the Jews of Hoof, a book this man had written. I had read it and hated the man before I had even met him. He had written that my Papa had left my Mutti and us children. Just that. He was a year younger than me and had gathered his information from many sources, some of them plain wrong. Yes, Papa had left Mutti and us children, because he had been sent to Dachau. This man had never mentioned the concentration camps. I had not realised that Herr Schunder was the same man who had written this rotten and untrue book. I kept my temper as best I could. According to his records of which he had many, two teenage boys had gone with my family in the cattle trucks to Riga. These boys had then been sent to a work camp. They had Russian surnames, so when the Russians liberated their camp, the boys had been returned to Kassel. This was in 1945. The war was over. All of Germany was feeling the guilt of what had happened to the Jewish people. Now many came forward to witness and remember. It must have been difficult not to notice a woman with six children. Of course they remembered what had happened. It had shocked them badly. As Mutti and the children came out of the cattle trucks, the monsters in charge wanted to separate Mutti from the children. Rolf, aged nearly eleven, (it was two weeks before his twelfth birthday) stood in front of my family with his arms outstretched and said, 'We are going to die, we will die together'. As soon as he had finished speaking, all my family were shot. This took place in December 1941, in Riga, Latvia.

No one can imagine my feelings on hearing these words,

words I felt to be true and would never be able to forget. I had spent all my adult life watching the horror films about concentration camps, watching in case I could see a brother or sister amongst these abused and wretched people. Thank God I had never succeeded in seeing any of them. I had imagined the greatest horrors happening to them. Now after all these years I felt great relief. They had travelled a terrible distance without food, water or any sanitary facilities but no other pain had been inflicted on them, and they had died, to me, a clean death. I could not stop crying, after all those years of imagining the horrors they might have endured. I pulled myself together to hear Herr Schunder asking me whether I would like a family tree of Mutti's family. He printed this out for me.

The telephone rang and he dashed out to answer. He returned to tell us we must go somewhere or other to meet the press who had come from Kassel. We three got into the car and the gear change business started again. We drove to a clearing in the woods where we found a large number of headstones. No graves just the stones. It appeared that the Catholic Church in Hoof had hidden these old stones amongst their own graves. After the war, the little reminder of old families had been set up in this clearing. To my dismay, a photographer and an interviewer arrived just as I found the gravestone of my great-great-grandmother. Somehow I had to answer questions put to me in German. Now I had to force myself to speak German again. To say I was distressed is putting it mildly. It was raining, I had just heard the fate of my family, now I found myself literally forced to speak a language I found abhorrent. So there I am standing in the rain being photographed by a gravestone of some one I have never heard of. While I can only concentrate on what I had been told about Mutti and the children. Nothing else mattered to me. Yet, I am being forced to distraction, by two men who I am sure meant well. Eventually they left me in peace. Not before the interviewer asked me in perfect English, where I lived. I could have cheerfully strangled him. It would have been no hardship for him to ask his questions in English. He had, however, followed his instructions. It had never occurred to him that I could not, or would not speak German. He was very apologetic, but it was too little, too late. I stood in the rain and once more mourned the loss of my dear ones.

As we returned to the car, I happened to mention a memory that had been with me all my life, the memory of the big house. Immediately Herr Schunder insisted that we visited this house. It was exactly as I had remembered it. It was now inhabited by the daughter of the old people I remembered. Of course they were old to me as a small child. We arrived unannounced but we were made very welcome. When the people were told who we were, they were overwhelmed. It was June and the gardens looked glorious. I mentioned a rose garden I remembered. The couple took me, each holding one of my hands, to see the garden; they were so amazed that I had remembered. Even more surprised when I asked where the walnut tree was? It appeared that this tree had fallen down not too many years before. How had I remembered this one tree when it stood at the edge of a forest. I could not explain how much that tree had meant to us children when we were very small. It had been a sanctuary in which we hid, a place to play, where no one would look for us. We so enjoyed the nuts this tree provided. How could I have forgotten?

We were treated to strawberries and cream. The men talked politics and the lady of the house (now a Bed and Breakfast establishment, it being too large for a private house) and I talked with difficulty about our children. We spent an hour or so there, were wished a safe journey home and left these hospitable people with arms full of roses and jars of strawberry jam.

In my memory, I had always imagined the village square to be enormous. Now we walked to the square; it was just big enough to hold four cars. How age distorts. On our way up to the square, we had passed a row of houses that had been rebuilt and were exactly alike. I stopped in front of one of the houses and asked our guide where the steps were? He looked at me in amazement.

Yes, he said, this was the place where my family had once lived. On rebuilding, the steps had been removed. I asked him if there was still a stream behind the house? This time he looked shocked. How could I have remembered the stream? He wasn't to know that to me the stream and Opa were synonymous, there was no way I could forget that stream. We returned to our guide's house. Before we left, he asked me if I would like to purchase the second book he had written? Being polite and finding no other way to thank him for his help, I bought the book. In the ten years since I was in Hoof have never opened his book. We returned to Kassel to see Esther and return her car, thank heavens intact. On the next day my companion and I returned to Heathrow. He to pick up his hired car and I to catch a coach home.

A week later my dear friend came to Swansea for a few days to meet Colin and reacquaint himself with a renewed city. I was so grateful to him: his company had made a terrible ordeal just about bearable. There are no circumstances that I can envisage that would make me return to Germany.

Later Years

IN 1997, I was approached by the local education department. They intended to bring the Anne Frank Exhibition to Swansea. For advertising purposes and to help with the exhibition, they wished me to help in any way possible. For many years our local paper had been writing articles about me, especially when it came to anything controversial, perhaps to do with a comment on the Holocaust or films like 'Schindler's List'. Over the years they had dubbed me the 'Survivor'. I was useful to advertise the exhibition.

When the Exhibition arrived in Swansea, many volunteers came forward to help show children and young people around and explain the meaning of the pictures. I was the only person who could actually say, 'I was there,' so found myself in great demand. The exhibition lasted four days a week for four weeks. It took about an hour to take twenty young people around the exhibition. The same group would then go into another room to see the Anne Frank video. Another group would immediately follow. This went on throughout each day. To my surprise, I found that adults were following each group. Listening to my explanation of all the pictures on display. One elderly couple waited until my group had gone into the other room, then the gentleman tentatively approached me. He wanted to ask some questions. He wanted to know whether I could forgive and forget what the German people had done to me and my family. Without thinking I told him that only God could forgive but I would never forget. I am sorry to say they were both in tears. My answers were spontaneous, but I had meant each word.

The reaction of the children and the young people to what they saw and what I was able to tell them was wonderful and very, very rewarding. They hung on my words and asked very relevant questions, waiting for the answers with great patience. Half way through the exhibition, I became ill. My arthritis had affected the bones in my head and I was more restricted than before and in great pain. However, there was no way this was going to stop me working with children I loved. Almost all my life since I came to Swansea I had had a sense of guilt. 'Why was I alive and all my brothers and sisters dead?' During the exhibition when the pain was all but unbearable, I finished taking my group around and went out to my car and sat there. Suddenly I found myself crying, not from pain. I heard a voice in my head saying, 'Now you must know why you are alive, you are the Teacher.' I was alone, so where was the voice coming from? With all that had happened to me throughout my life, I had never faltered in my strong faith in God. Was this His way of bringing home to me what I had to do?

Since that time, I have visited many schools telling my story to children and young people. By 2003 I had lectured to almost seven thousand children. Add to this the adult groups to which I have gone and the number of people I have spoken to becomes many more. I accept no money for what I do. When adult groups insist on payment, it goes to my favourite charity, Childline. Had this charity been around in my teen years, perhaps my life would have been a little different. I would have had someone to talk to.

My love of children has never wavered. Still I must tell them of the horrors of my past life. It is the only way I can make them understand the importance of what to avoid in the future. I explain to them how abhorrent discrimination is in all its forms, race, colour, religion, that differences are merely on the surface. Underneath, we are all God's children regardless of the differences. I explain the horrors of bullies. They start small and if not forced to change, eventually they turn into dictators, not named Hitler, but Davies, Jones or Thomas. I make it a point to explain to them that a Holocaust can, and has happened in other places, for instance Kosova, Rwanda, many other countries in their lifetime. Unless the present and future generations do something about these horrors, who will be left to enjoy a free and happy life. I insist that I, the past, ask them, the future, to make sure that peace will reign in their time and in the future.

When I first started talking to young people, I was very nervous and uncertain whether they understood the message I was trying to convey. Soon letters started to arrive from schools, addressed to me. I was amazed, thrilled and delighted at their content. The letters are still arriving, they make it clear that my message was received and understood in ways that went beyond my wildest expectations. Please God, I hope to continue visiting schools as long as I am physically able.

This is the first year of the Holocaust Memorial Day. In my opinion, this should have taken place fifty years ago. It has happened now and will I pray continue each year. If in years to come people will react the way they have this year, the Holocaust will not just be remembered on one day of the year, but through-out each day of each week throughout the year. The pictures I have planted in the hearts of the people I have had the privilege to speak to, will I hope and trust, remain for all time to come. I pray for the strength to carry on what is to me a God given task as long as I am physically able.

Time passes. I received a telephone call from a lady who had come from Munich. She had come to Britain to do research for a book she was writing about the Kindertransport. Bertha Leverson had given her my name and phone number insisting that I was one of the Kinder that should be interviewed. I agreed to go to London to meet her. When she met my coach at Victoria Station, we made a very odd pair. I am very short and she must have been almost six foot tall. We went to the Wiener Library, the only place we could be alone and quiet. She set up her recording equipment and I talked for two hours. She was delighted. Some days later, she phoned me to thank me for giving her my time and information. She went on to tell me that she had visited a Refugee office. There she was shown a pile of documents dated 1939 which had been taken from London during the war and stored for safe keeping in a garage outside the city. They had just come to light. She went on to tell me that the very first docu-ment, an exit permit, was mine and had my photograph on it. She gave me the name and address where this document was being held. When I wrote asking about it, I was rewarded with the exit permit I should have had with me when entering Britain in 1939. Up to this time, I had never had an official document, so I really officially never existed.

Some months later I received the monthly news letter which had been published ever since our first reunion in 1989. On the cover were three photographs. To my astonishment, one was mine. Readers were asked if they recognised themselves, to please write to Bertha who had documents relating to the photographs. When my document arrived I was delighted to find it was my Entry Permit for G.B. Now after all those years, I was truly official, I had papers.

In 1999 the Kindertransport arranged the 60th and last Reunion. Many of the people from the 50th reunion had of course died; their children would be allowed to attend instead. This event took place in part of the London University. Opposite was a large hotel which served Kosher food should this be required. It was a very different event from the 1989 reunion. This one was over organised and very formal. Not in any way as enjoyable as the first one. To my joy, my Australian friend was invited to take part in the event. We stayed together in a hotel in Golders Green. On the first day, after the official opening, there were symposiums, group discussions and many other events. My friend and I went to different events in different buildings then met for lunch. After lunch we would again part to do our own thing. During the first day, I was approached by a young couple from Kassel who were not part of the reunion. They wanted to make videos of the members from Kassel. Dorrith was the first to be videoed, Henny was not present, she had just lost Peter her husband and was not up to taking part. Next day, it was my turn. It was difficult to find a quiet place. Eventually a room was found that was suitable. I was interviewed, at least it started as an interview, but soon became me telling my story as I had done many times before. I spoke for an hour which seemed to please my interviewers.

The three days flew very quickly. The third day was to be a picnic. My friend and I decided that we would forgo this and spend the day together. We walked around London, just enjoying each other's company. Bought pounds of cherries, a fruit we both loved. Next morning I had to return to Swansea. We parted with great sadness, at our ages it was improbable that we would meet again. During our two meetings we had put forty five years into eight days. Five in Germany, three in England. We still stay in touch, by e-mail of course, and an occasional telephone call. With the time difference between Australia and Britain, each time the telephone rang at some unearthly hour, Colin used to say 'This must be your friend'.

Riga

I BELONG to an organisation called AJR, the Association of Jewish Refugees. Each month a newsletter is published and sent to members. In June 2001 an article appeared in the Newsletter which spoke of a Memorial that was being completed in memory of the Jewish men, women and children who had been sent by cattle truck to Riga and subsequently shot. There had never been such a memorial before.

What I mean is that there are memorials to the dead of concentration camps and to the atrocities found therein. But there hasn't been a memorial to those poor souls who for no reason, except their religion, were heartlessly and mercilessly shot. Before June 2001, I hadn't even known where Riga was; I do not even know whether I wanted to know. Now everything changed. At last, it was possible for me to actually know where my family were buried. The article went on to say that if anyone wanted to attend the ceremony of dedication they should contact a Mr. E. Herzl in Vienna who had been working for many years with the Germans and Austrians and the Eastern countries to make this dream of a memorial come true. For months he and I corresponded by e-mail. He too had come via the Kindertransport to Britain in 1938 and had spent some years here. I also wrote a letter to be published in the Newsletter, telling people of my circumstances and asking if anyone else would like to make the trip. I was seventy and not in the best of health. This was not a journey one could make alone. After the letter was published, my telephone started ringing. Two ladies in their 80s wished to join me on this journey. First, however, they were making a journey to Israel, then to Vienna. On their return they would contact me. Within minutes, another phone call. This time from an eighty-one year old gentleman,

Garvis, from Sale, in Cheshire. He had been so touched by my letter that he could not bear the thought of my going alone. He was due to have dialysis, but would put this off to a later date.

I was deeply moved at the thought of an elderly, ill man making such an effort on my behalf. Over the next few weeks, Norbert and I spent hours on the phone. It was like talking to an older brother. I was delighted to tell him of the two ladies who intended to accompany me which put his mind at rest.

Erich Herzl and I were still corresponding. Eventually, he sent me a list which contained addresses of people who wanted more information. I wrote to each one and received many replies. Very few were physically able to make such a journey. One lady from Birmingham, whose name was Eva Lorimer, asked me for details of accommodation and other costs involved. I too admitted that I was worried about costs, especially for accommodation. I received another letter from a couple who lived in London. They wanted to join Eva and me in what had now become a pilgrimage. Eva and I wrote many letters and had long telephone conversations. Eventually, we decided to share a room, this being the cheapest option although we hadn't met each other.

Travelling from Swansea to Gatwick is not a comfortable journey. Nevertheless, as always I arrived early and walked around the terminal, looking for another lost soul. I had numerous cups of tea, anything to waste time, of which I had a great deal to spare. After some hours, I felt a presence at my side. I turned and the lady standing besides me simultaneously turned to me. We spoke each other's names. Eva and I had met, like homing pigeons, not knowing one another, but drawn together. We knew that we would make good friends and companions.

We found our seats in the crowded plane. Flying to a destination to which we all needed to go. We arrived in the early hours of Friday the 30th December. At the airport, a mini bus met us and drove us to the Riga. Despite our being cold and very tired, it was impossible not to admire this beautiful hotel where we were shown to our rooms and brought trays of tea and biscuits. We were warm for the first time since leaving the plane. Eva and I were too tired to shower. We went straight to our beds and tried hard to sleep. We knew we would have a hard day in front of us, although we had no idea how hard.

We must have slept for we both awoke very early. After breakfast, we discussed with our companions where to go next. Our
instructions were very sketchy. We started by finding the synagogue and asked questions until we found someone who knew
where we were to go. Unfortunately, none of us had a very good
sense of direction and soon we were lost once more. Finally,
more by luck than judgement, we found the Hall where the ceremony was taking place. Some of the speeches were in Latvian.
To my surprise the speeches in German I could understand. At
last, the speeches finished and some thousand people congregated in another hall where refreshments were available. We four,
probably looking quite lost, felt very much out of place. We were
the only people who could not speak German, the predominant
language we heard about us.

Soon there was a mass exodus to the coaches parked outside.
People were pushing to get seats. We set off through a strange
landscape of derelict looking apartment blocks. The only time I
had ever seen their like was on television, when they showed
either Russian or East European countries. The poverty was
palpable, the shabbiness could not be hidden. No door or window
had been repainted for years. The journey seemed endless. Then
finally, we were at the edge of a forest, Bikernieki, where the
coaches turned off the main road and took a right into a marked
lane, just wide enough for the vehicles. There was a large sign-
post. I could not read it as we sped past. Had the coach lost its
way? Eventually we followed someone who looked as if he knew
what to do. We stopped in a very large clearing. Very like the
amphitheatres of old. In the middle was the memorial, the reason
for our coming. It consisted of a tall, very plain, yet beautiful arch.
Everyone tried to find a spot from which to find the best view.
About a thousand people stood on some eight inches of ice.
There was an awesome stillness.

The master of ceremony (for want of a better name) introduced the dignitaries who said Kaddish, the prayers for the
departed, prayers that are spoken constantly in synagogues and

by people such as myself in remembrance of our lost ones. Then the President of Latvia spoke. First in Latvian and then in English, one of the few English speakers at the ceremony. Speech followed speech making little impression on me. Then representatives from Austria and the Eastern Countries, from towns who had sent men, women and children. As it was going on, I thought there was something wrong with me. I could not cry; I looked about me and found that no-one was crying. The pain was so great and our thoughts so dreadful. If the others were like me, all I could see and think about were the faces of my mother, brothers and sisters. Beloved faces I had not seen and who had been dead for sixty years. They were so clear to me. The pain so great, my tears were drowning my heart, not my eyes. Over the years I had felt pain. But this pain was beyond belief. I prayed that the ground would open up and swallow me, perhaps then I would stop hurting.

The ceremony seemed to go on and on. Then the representative from Kassel was announced. I knew that the scroll in her hand contained the names of Johanna, Rolf, Heinz, Sally, Ruth, Ludwig and Zilla Wertheim. All my family. I thought the pain I had felt previously was bad. The pain I felt at that moment was beyond bearing. I cursed the God, my own personal God, with whom I had always had such a wonderful relationship. The God who had given me the strength to survive so much, who had given me such strength. At that moment I no longer believed in Him. I had come to this place to lay down my burden of grief. Instead, I had picked up the burden of 25,000 people who were buried in mass graves in this awful place.

The ceremony finished at last. People went in all directions. I found that someone was asking for me by name. It was Erich Hertz. The man, who had been very kind to me, and with whom I had corresponded by e-mail for such a long time. This very man, who had worked for years to make this memorial possible. Erich and I spoke for a couple of minutes. He was one of the important people everyone wanted to meet. Eva and I found small stone gardens; rocks formed a border, making each a separate entity. Each bore the name of one of the towns from where the mourners had come. She found Hamburg where she had come from. I found Kassel, the nearest town to my village. We wandered the forest and found many mounds of heaped earth covered in snow. Despite walking with a stick, Eva and I climbed each small hill. These were the mass graves of the 250,000 who had died in this forest. On top of each mound, I said Yiskar, another prayer for the dead. I had no idea in which of these places my family were buried, but that place was here somewhere. I said my prayer on each hill, thinking 'If this one holds the remains of my family, so be it. If it is someone else's family, a prayer for others is just as important, someone may have prayed over my family'.

I have no idea how many hours passed before we were herded back into the coaches. Again, we made the return journey through the desolate landscape, back to the town of Riga. As we were about to reach our destination, small booklets relating to different towns were handed out. I had missed the representative for Kassel. The coach with this lady had already arrived in the town sometime before. After a great deal of walking through narrow streets, I found the hotel and the lady from Kassel who had been looking for me, without success. There was only one other person from my town and he spoke only German and I could not understand what he tried to say to me. I spent some hours with the lady from Kassel. As I was going, I asked her for my copy of the scroll. Unfortunately, she only had her own copy, but she let me scrutinise it to find my family. How could she have thought I could not find a whole page with the name Wertheim. Once I had this parchment in my hands I found I was unwilling to return it to her. Thankfully she understood what I was feeling. We spoke for a while longer. She was interested in what I knew of the fate of my family. She, it seemed, knew very little except that they had died in Riga.

Eventually, I made my way back to my hotel where Eva reminded me that we had not eaten since breakfast. I felt as if I would never want to eat again. My companion, ever the sensible one, persuaded me that we should find somewhere to eat. Our hotel was quite near to the centre of the town. We gingerly made our way to what we thought must be a large restaurant, only to find this was a theatre. Not very far from the theatre was the smallest restaurant I had ever seen. We went to the counter where food was displayed. I have written of poverty on the outskirts of the town, now we saw it in the food displayed. By pointing, we managed to select something that looked edible that turned out to be a cabbage tart. The most expensive item on the menu, it tasted of cabbage and little else. After barely drinkable tea, we wandered the streets, careful where we trod on the pavements that were like banks of ice. The poverty of the place showed itself in ever shop and little roadside stall. This was no place for visitors, too cold, too bleak with very little to offer in the way of entertainment. We made our way back to the hotel, mainly to get warm. Neither of us had ever experienced such cold. We went to our room thinking to be company for one another. There were no words to express what we had endured in the forest. It was no use trying to read, nothing could take the sights we had seen out of our minds.

We spoke instead of our past lives. I told her of my experiences since arriving in Britain. She told me of hers. I thought I had had a tough time. By comparison to Eva, I had lived in the lap of luxury. She had been six when she came over on the Kindertransport. She came to the family of a Church of England Minister with three children of their own. Two younger and a boy older than Eva. It appeared they were very mischievous. Any trouble they caused, they blamed on Eva. She spent her life being blamed for things she had not done. Forever trying to avoid the other children. I believe she had been sent away to a boarding school, and eventually to the Jewish Refugee Committee who financed her College education. She became a teacher. The abuses she suffered in her English home were dreadful and left their mark on her.

We talked of our respective lives and every subject under the sun. What we could not talk about was the time spent in the

Bikernieki forest. Later in the evening, in the hotel restaurant, I could not concentrate on food. My thoughts were filled with the mass graves. The only thought that kept me sane was the fact that at last I had seen or walked over my family's graves. Prior to this visit, I had no idea where Riga was, where they had died or where they were buried. Now at least there was a grave, one of many, but I had walked there and knew where they were buried. It was a strange consolation, but a consolation nevertheless. Eventually out of desperation, Eva and I went to our beds, hoping to sleep. From childhood I had never managed to sleep without medication, so I took my pills. It was of no use. All my life I have not been able to contemplate sleep, without saying my prayers. I said them. Firstly apologising for my cursing Him, then my normal nightly prayer. This was a ritual that normally calms me and gives my pills a chance to work. Once again, I became calmer and slept for a short time. Eva too seemed to have slept.

After breakfast, we went to the square, not far from our hotel. There once again were coaches. This time only three of them, I was very confused about what day this was. We had flown from Gatwick on Thursday night, arriving Friday early morning. We had spent Friday at the reception and in the Bikernieke forest. Now it was Saturday. The coaches took us through almost the same dreadful landscape to the Ghettos. Dreadful places. Now ruins. But enough was left to enable those with a little imagination, to see what horrors they represented.

The streets, if that was what they had been, were, I think, named after the towns from which the inhabitants had come. My recollection is vague on this matter. There were two people who had survived this ghetto and the subsequent slaughter. They explained to us the horrors, the dreadful conditions in which the people had had to live. The lack of food and sanitation, the freezing cold, lack of clothes. Why had the organisers bothered to put us through yet another hell, imagining the horrors and the suffering of people now long dead. I refused to walk any further and closed my ears to further talk. Enough was enough. My

family had not had to go through the horrors of these ghettos. I
was almost glad that they had died when they died and not had
to suffer these horrors which the survivors with great courage
told us about.

After what seemed many hours, we returned to the coaches
and were driven to yet another forest. This one was called
Rumbula. Here again were mass graves. 30,000 people were
buried there, women and children mainly, from the Slovak countries. How can one area hold so much horror? Had we not hurt
enough the previous day? Why did we have to walk on yet more
mass graves? Yes, they meant more pain, but we who had come
from Germany and Austria had had our fill of pain the day
before. Eventually we returned to the centre of Riga.

Walking across the square later, we saw a notice of a concert
to be held that evening. We truly did not want entertainment, but
what was there to do for a long evening and another day. We
decided to go to the concert, if we could find the hall. The staff
at the hotel were ever helpful and most spoke excellent English.
They found us a map of the town and showed us where the
Concert Hall was. Outside it was dark and except for Christmas
lights the streets were badly lit. Eventually we found the building
and, with two more companions, we sat entranced by the
Latvian National Orchestra playing music that we knew. Played
so beautifully. For two hours, we were able to lose ourselves in
the music. What a joyous two hours. After at a restaurant, we
enjoyed good food and a glass of wine and made conversation,
about our families, children, grandchildren. We talked about any
subject barring the one in all our minds. Yes, we had an enjoyable
evening. Yet we all knew that our memories could not be blotted
out then nor in the days, months and years to come. We returned
to our hotel and went to our rooms, once again hoping to sleep.

Before going to Riga, I had met through another friend and
via the e-mail a woman who lived there. Her name was Lilita. We
corresponded for some months before my journey, and agreed
that I would send her Sterling which she would exchange for Lats
(Latvian money). I therefore was the only member of our party

to have Latvian cash. We had arranged that I would telephone her when I knew my plans and invite her to meet me for tea at the hotel where I was staying. She came on the Sunday afternoon. I had had no idea what she looked like. I had described myself to her as small with grey/white hair. We met at the bar and immediately became friends.

Her English was more than good, it was perfect. I was not surprised when she told me that she was an interpreter. We talked of Latvia and her parents. She still lived at home. The poverty I had noticed was a fact of life, though Lilita told me that things were much improved since the Russians had left. I hate to think what it had been like before. A working man earned £150 per month. She earned more, because she worked for a foreign company, still she did not earn enough to afford a flat of her own. We spent a pleasant few hours together. We must have looked an odd pair. I am 5.2 feet tall and she must have been at least six inches taller than me. We have stayed friends through e-mail.

Time had seemed to stand still for Eva and me. We explored the town, getting lost with monotonous regularity. Did some window shopping, amazed at the low prices of the goods we saw. When we came across a supermarket, with the little money we had left, we purchased small things, nuts and some chocolates which Eva wanted as gifts, at unbelievable prices to us foreigners. We went to the restaurant in the hotel for our last meal there. This time we enjoyed it, we were hungry, and it was almost time to return home. Early next morning, we were woken by a maid laden with two trays; each contained a pot of tea, some toast and jam. The time was about 4 a.m. The mini bus that had brought us four days before, now returned us to the airport where everything was closed, except one little stall selling tea or coffee. We had cup after cup of tea in this bleak, ugly building. Our flight did not leave until 7 a.m. The plane's engine had firstly to be de-iced which may give you some idea how cold it was in Latvia. At long last we took off. I left that dreary and hurtful country without regret. I was pleased that I had gone; it was something I had to do. But I was thankful to arrive in Gatwick. Time wise, almost before we had set out from Riga. I said my goodbyes to our London couple. Eva and I had to wait for our respective coaches. She to Birmingham, I to Swansea. My coach came minutes before hers. We did not say goodbye. We had no intention of losing touch. Except for a rather longish period, when time did not permit it, we have spoken on the phone and written letters. Such friends are too valuable to lose.

Colin

COLIN MET ME AS ALWAYS. Why did he look at me so strangely? I asked him the reason, but he was evasive, not like Colin at all. We arrived home some thirty minutes later. As usual when I have been away, on my return, the first thing Colin does, is to make me a cup of tea, a ritual. He asked me how the journey had gone, how I had coped with the cold and the country, but no personal questions. My husband not known for his reticence, now avoided asking personal questions. I managed to get through the day. Exhausted, aching (had walked too much) tired to my very bones. In the early evening he suggested that for once I should go to bed early. He insisted. Reluctantly, I took all my pills, going to bed without any hope of sleep.

When I awoke, I looked at my clock and could not see it clearly. I felt very strange and disorientated. I knew I was home and in bed, but everything looked strange and out of focus. Colin came to see if I was awake. His shocked expression told me that something was wrong. With his help, I went to the bathroom. One look in the mirror told me all I needed, not wanted, to know. During the night I had had a small stroke. My right eye had dropped quite badly and the right side of my face was distorted. No wonder my husband looked at me strangely. He had always had a terrible fear that I would die before him, and he would be left on his own. Now, he thought his fear justified. At our surgery, the doctor confirmed what we already knew. When I asked how long this distortion might last, he told me it could go tomorrow or stay for a while. This was small comfort. I did not want to leave the house, even though I felt better. Colin kept telling me that with my glasses on, no-one would notice the distortion.

Now two years later, the distortion has not gone. Yes, it is better, first thing in the morning and for the first few hours of the day. But my right eye does not open properly and drags the right side of my face down. I have had to have a prism put into the right lens of my glasses. I did not realise at the time, that I had been either asleep or unconscious, for twenty-four hours. This I think must have frightened my husband more than anything else.

As I had promised, I wrote to everyone who had been in touch with me regarding the Memorial. With great difficulty, I described all I had seen and felt. Giving details of the actual arch and the agony of watching the handing over and the scrolls. There was not point in trying to gloss over what I had seen and felt. The truth had to be told. I received many replies thanking me for taking the trouble. It had been painful, but some of the people to whom I wrote, would never have the chance to see or feel what was so important to all of us.

Some months after my return, I received a telephone call from Erich Herzl in Vienna. He told me that he had put my name forward to attend an International Conference in Berlin. I thanked him for the thought, but there was no way I would return to Germany no matter for what purpose. He understood my feelings and that was that. He phones now and then to keep in touch. When I was well enough, I wrote to the editor of the AJR(the magazine in which I had found the article about the memorial) asking him to publish an article I had written about my experiences in Riga. There was no reply for some time. Then Erich phoned me again. The AJR had asked him for an article about the Riga memorial. Knowing that I had already written something, he suggested they printed the article they had received already from me. He was most irate. In the next issue of the newsletter, they printed my article in full. Again I received phone calls from people who had read my first letter, thanking me for making the occasion so real for them.

About three months later, I received a letter from the Mayor of Kassel, inviting me to come to the Dedication Ceremony of the new synagogue. He emphasised that all my expenses would be paid in full, including flight, accommodation etc. I knew that my two friends were going. Henny from Birmingham and Dorrith from Scotland. They had tried very hard to persuade me to come with them. I wrote to the Mayor of Kassel informing him that as much as I would love to be at the Dedication of the new synagogue, I could not think of a single reason that would make me return to the city which had sent my family to their death. I wished all the visitors who were attending well. What I was not prepared for was the video they made of the occasion. They had taken items I had made in a video in 1999 in London. Both Henny and Dorrith spoke to a large audience including all the city dignitaries. I was also told by Dorrith that my letter had been read out and translated at this civic gathering. I have no regrets at my refusal. I still receive periodic letters from Kassel, but as they are in German, they are dispatched into my dustbin. My loss is too great. There is no way Kassel can make reparation to me in any form for the lives they dispatched to Riga and the consequent deaths.

June the 10th 2003 and I am bringing my story up to date. The last three months have been absolute hell. On the 7th of March, without any warning, my Colin died. At eighty-four, he had only been in hospital once in his life, a matter of two days. Now he was very frightened. He had no idea what was happening around him. Tubes and needles coming out of his body. He could not turn or move; there was always someone wanting more blood or to test something else. Colin had always had a horror of needles. Now I do not think he even felt them. I sat for nine hours holding his hand. Every time I let go, the monitor would go crazy. So I sat holding his hand, talking, talking. Every day. Conversations we had not had for a long time. The doctors and nurses worked around me. I phoned Paul, Colin's son, Jean and Ron. I asked the latter not to come to the hospital, but they came nevertheless. Soon after Paul and Eira (his wife) came, the doctor came to see us. He explained that Colin was fading fast. He suggested that we go home for a while. There was nothing more we could do and soon he was to be moved to intensive care and put on a life support machine. Paul and I went once more to see him. He spoke to Paul. Not knowing how ill he was, he asked after Eira and Jack (Jack is our ten year old grandson). He asked how work was going? Suddenly, he turned to me, squeezing my hand. His last words to me were 'Thank you so much for looking after me'.

We returned after about an hour and a half. There was no Colin. This unmoving man, hooked up to a machine was not my husband. I sat with him throughout the night. When Paul returned in the morning, the doctor in charge, with our permission, took what had been Colin off the life support system. I had phoned Anita the night before telling her that Colin was in hospital. She immediately said she was coming. I begged her to wait until we knew more. She arrived thirty minutes after Colin had been disconnected from the life support machine. She insisted on seeing him, but I did not want her to see the strange person my Colin had become. She took one look at the Colin she loved so much and burst into tears. I had cried throughout the night and thought there could not possibly be more tears to shed.

My dearest daughter arranged to stay with me for a couple of days. Her way of dealing with things is to clean it if it stands still. As I had not slept for twenty-four hours, she insisted that I take my pills and go to bed. When I awoke, I found she had been out shopping looking for something to make me eat. Strange since I have the reputation of having enough food in both my cupboards and freezers to feed the Welsh Regiment. A standing joke to Colin and all my friends.

Never, never, had I envisaged his death. Now-a-days, eighty-four is no age. As far as we knew, he had been feeling a little weak other than that, he was well. He did not even look his age. I did not know that the death of someone dear to me could hurt so much. We spent hours together, not saying a word. Colin would not wear his hearing aid. As long as I was with him, he was content to live in the world of the television and crossword books. Now, my life, the house is empty. Everything too tidy. Grief has become my enemy. I tackle everyday tasks. I have spent months putting official papers in order. Writing dozens of letter to change things into my name. Even papers in joint names have to be altered. This has kept me busy. I still cook at luncheon club. Lecturing to adults, I am rarely idle. Idleness gives too much time to think. Most of my life I have mourned my mother, brothers and sisters. This is different. I spent nearly 35 years with Colin. Two weeks after he died would have been our 31st Wedding Anniversary. We had, however, been together four years before we married. This grieving is very different. I have cried till my eyes are sore, nothing helps. This was the man who encouraged me to write this book. Each time I came upstairs to this computer, I would say 'I am going up for an hour'. Three hours later, I would look at my watch and find the time had flown. Each time Colin would say 'I know how difficult this book is for you to write, so when you start and get busy, I do not feel it right to disturb you. I made myself a sandwich'. Although many ways an exasperating man, obstinate and selfish man, yet when he does not want to disturb me when I am writing, I forget all the faults he had, after all we all have them. I miss him in so many little ways. For more than sixty years I have mourned my family. I keep asking the Lord what dreadful thing have I done to deserve so much pain. So far, no answer.

However, I have my children and grandchildren. I love them dearly and that love is, thank God, returned. They are healthy, loving and loved. This has to be enough for me.